W9-BXG-375

*Praise for*
# BETWEEN A ROCK
# AND A GRACE PLACE

In *Between a Rock and a Grace Place*, Carol Kent has written a gem of a book which will be a great help to those who face seemingly insurmountable hurdles. I faced such a dilemma when I was under investigation after Watergate. Carol faced it when her son was charged with murder. It is then that we placed ourselves in the hands of Jesus. This book recounts the stories of others who have found peace in Jesus in trying times and includes beautiful Scriptures that illuminate the love Jesus has for each of us.

> CHUCK COLSON, founder of Prison Fellowship and the
> Colson Center for Biblical Worldview

✦ ✦ ✦

Throughout the pages of *Between a Rock and a Grace Place*, Carol Kent opens her heart and pours out the rich lessons she's learned in the hard places of life. Because she loves people and because she loves Jesus, Carol holds nothing back, letting us experience her joys and sorrows right along with her, helping us discover deep truths we can apply to our own challenging situations. Poignant letters from her incarcerated son and moving stories from other sojourners who've crossed this family's path give a clear message of hope: God's grace shines even in the darkest corners.

> LIZ CURTIS HIGGS, bestselling author of *Bad Girls of the Bible*

✦ ✦ ✦

I have loved the Kent family for many years, but I will never get over how God has used them to assure all of us that he can use any tragedy in a redeeming way. Carol is like Jesus in her storytelling. We first think these stories are about others' lives; then we realize they are about our own.

> DR. JOEL C. HUNTER, senior pastor of Northland,
> A Church Distributed, Longwood, Florida

*Between a Rock and a Grace Place* is riveting. Carol Kent compels us to revisit our own stories as she weaves her personal heartaches and hard places with insights and principles to bring hope when life's circumstances can seem unbearable. She helps me believe that God's grace is sufficient for all of my needs.

> DEVI TITUS, president of Global Pastors' Wives Network and coleader of Kingdom Global Ministries

✣ ✣ ✣

*Between a Rock and a Grace Place* reminds all of us to look for divine surprises in the middle of challenging circumstances. Carol Kent has discovered that grace grows best when life doesn't offer easy answers. She has experienced freedom on the inside and profound joy in the middle of an impossible situation. This book is filled with refreshment, authenticity, and hope. Don't miss it!

> DR. TIM CLINTON, president of the American Association of Christian Counselors

✣ ✣ ✣

Carol Kent has traveled roads few of us have. As a result she is able to take us on a journey filled with grace, power, and healing. Read this book. It is a divine surprise.

> KATHY TROCCOLI, singer, author, speaker

✣ ✣ ✣

Tight places provoke claustrophobia — the natural urge to find a way to escape. Carol Kent knows tight spaces, deep binds, and the panic they induce. Yet she has been shaped by the narrow way to know the life-giving breath that comes when God opens a way of life in the face of our deepest surprises. This is a glorious book in which to find the breath of God and the ample passageway of his love.

> DAN B. ALLENDER, PhD, professor of counseling at Mars Hill Graduate School, Seattle, and author of *The Wounded Heart*

✣ ✣ ✣

Carol Kent has great insight, a growing understanding of God's grace, and an amazing story. *Between a Rock and a Grace Place* captures all three. No one would choose her journey, but I can't imagine anyone walking in her shoes with more generosity of heart and spirit. She invites us to walk with her through the joy and heartache. As we do, we see an amazing grace.

MARY GRAHAM, president of Women of Faith

⊹ ⊹ ⊹

The call to follow Christ is so counterintuitive that I sometimes wonder if we can only hear it clearly in suffering. If so, Carol Kent is a chosen mouthpiece to make clear God's call to trust him in very dark places, to understand and actually know joy in agony of soul, and to love others in the worst moments of life. *Between a Rock and a Grace Place* incarnates what's centrally good about the good news of Christ, the truth I'm yearning to grasp and communicate.

DR. LARRY CRABB, founder and
director of NewWay Ministries

⊹ ⊹ ⊹

I have known Carol and Gene for many years and have followed their journey into the deep valley of heartache and loss. Now you can read about their journey up the steep hill toward hope and grace. You'll be gripped by the reality of what they have endured, and yet grateful that God's mercy is best seen against the backdrop of human failure and broken dreams. Read this book and pass it along to a friend.

DR. ERWIN W. LUTZER, senior pastor
of The Moody Church, Chicago

⊹ ⊹ ⊹

What a God-story! In Carol Kent's new book she eloquently shares that Jesus is the source of hope, comfort, compassion, freedom, joy, love, and limitless grace. I was profoundly moved as I read Jason Kent's letters. His life is making an eternal difference in the lives of forsaken and forgotten people. *Between a Rock and a Grace Place* proclaims this powerful truth: no matter where we find ourselves, Jesus is THERE. What an inspiration this book is!

FERN NICHOLS, president and founder
of Moms In Touch International (www.MomsInTouch.org)

⊹ ⊹ ⊹

This is my kind of book — it's real! Carol Kent offers no pat answers. No easy fixes. She speaks authentically as one who stands *Between a Rock and a Grace Place* because that is where she is living. In the midst of darkness, heartache, pain, and unanswered questions she speaks honestly about her own struggle to find that grace place. There's not a happy ending. Not all the questions are answered, but she finds enduring truths that God gives in our darkness.

RUTH GRAHAM, speaker and author

✤ ✤ ✤

For the first time, Jason Kent speaks from his heart in letters to his parents about fear, wrong choices, sin, repentance, punishment, and hard lessons learned in the middle of a maximum security prison. Carol Kent skillfully takes his words and tells the story of their family's lost hopes, new choices, and a different kind of joy in a not-to-be-missed book about redemption, forgiveness, and the grace that can be experienced when we press into the Rock!

JULIE CLINTON, president of Extraordinary Women and author of *A Woman's Path to Emotional Freedom*

✤ ✤ ✤

Once again Carol Kent has shown us how to live in the midst of shattered dreams and random pain — and to find redemption and purpose by choosing to embrace all of God's surprises. *Between a Rock and a Grace Place* reminds me to continually cling to the Rock of Ages so that I, too, might discover with Carol that "the best gifts in life come disguised in suffering I would never choose, but they are precious."

LUCINDA SECREST McDOWELL, author of *Amazed by Grace* (www.EncouragingWords.net)

✤ ✤ ✤

How would I react if my only child were in prison for life? How much harder could a wilderness journey be? And yet, just as God gave the Israelites water in the wilderness, so grace is pouring into the lives of Carol, Gene, and their son, J.P. How heartened I was by J.P.'s letters — his determination "not to waste prison"! I identified with Carol's meltdown in her closet — and sighed at the grace that came. I understood the grief Gene felt when he compared his son's circumstances to the circumstances of his friend's son. Yet Gene is determined not to waste his pain. Carol, Gene, and J.P. — your pain isn't being wasted. God is using your stories to give us hope, to give us water from the Rock.

DEE BRESTIN, author of *The God of All Comfort*

✤ ✤ ✤

Rarely do I find a nonfiction book to be a page-turner. But this one is. Carol continues sharing her painfully raw story wrapped in a grace-filled hope that few of us know but all of us need. While I've never experienced the same heartbreak as hers, the advice and teaching in this book will be a treasure I'll refer to for years to come.

LYSA TERKEURST, president of Proverbs 31 Ministries and author of *Becoming More than a Good Bible Study Girl* (she blogs daily at www.LysaTerKeurst.com)

✤ ✤ ✤

No longer will I express my helplessness by saying, "I'm stuck between a rock and a hard place." After reading Carol Kent's personal insights, her friends' stories, and biblical examples of those who experienced divine surprises, I can now confidently and expectantly respond to my tight places by proclaiming, "I'm secure because I'm between the Rock and a grace place." Thank you, Carol.

CYNTHIA HEALD, author of *Becoming a Woman of Excellence*

✤ ✤ ✤

Are you walking on a rocky path thinking, *I can handle the hard spots of life on my own* — no help needed? Or are you stumbling on the slippery gravel of questions and fearful feelings of anguish and despair? Stop! Your solution is in this book. It will take your heart from being stoned by the sharp pebbles of life to becoming strengthened by the Rock of all ages.

THELMA WELLS, D.D., president of A Woman of God Ministries (www.thelmawells.com)

# CAROL KENT

Bestselling Author of *When I Lay My Isaac Down*

# BETWEEN A ROCK AND A GRACE PLACE

## DIVINE SURPRISES IN THE TIGHT SPOTS OF LIFE

ZONDERVAN®

ZONDERVAN.com/
AUTHORTRACKER
*follow your favorite authors*

ZONDERVAN

*Between a Rock and a Grace Place*
Copyright © 2010 by Carol Kent

This title is also available as a Zondervan ebook. Visit www.zondervan.com/ebooks.

This title is also available in a Zondervan audio edition. Visit www.zondervan.fm.

Requests for information should be addressed to:

Zondervan, *Grand Rapids, Michigan 49530*

Library of Congress Cataloging-in-Publication Data

Kent, Carol, 1947–
    Between a rock and a grace place : divine surprises in the tight spots of life / Carol
Kent.
       p.  cm.
    Includes bibliographical references.
    ISBN 978-0-310-33098-1 (hardcover, jacketed)
    1. Grace (Theology). 2. Consolation. I. Title.
BT761.3.K46  2010
248.8'6 – dc22                                                   2010023776

All Scripture quotations, unless otherwise indicated, are taken from *The Message.* Copyright © 1993, 1994, 1995, 1996, 2000, 2001, 2002. Used by permission of NavPress Publishing Group.

Scripture quotations marked NLT are taken from the *Holy Bible, New Living Translation,* copyright © 1996, 2004. Used by permission of Tyndale House Publishers, Inc., Wheaton, Illinois 60189. All rights reserved.

Scripture quotations marked NIV are taken from the Holy Bible, *New International Version®, NIV®.* Copyright © 1973, 1978, 1984 by Biblica, Inc.™ Used by permission of Zondervan. All rights reserved worldwide.

Scripture quotations marked NASB are taken from the *New American Standard Bible.* Copyright © 1960, 1962, 1963, 1968, 1971, 1972, 1973, 1975, 1977, 1995 by The Lockman Foundation. Used by permission.

Scripture quotations marked KJV are taken from the King James Version of the Bible.

*Cover design: Curt Diepenhorst*
*Cover photography: Shutterstock® Images*
*Interior design: Beth Shagene*

*Printed in the United States of America*

10 11 12 13 14 15 /DCI/ 24 23 22 21 20 19 18 17 16 15 14 13 12 11 10 9 8 7 6 5 4 3 2 1

*To my parents,*
*Clyde and Pauline Afman.*

*Thank you for consistently pressing into the Rock*
*and reminding me to find the place of safety and grace*
*in the middle of my darkest hours.*

*I love you.*

"Careful! I've put a huge stone on the road to Mount Zion,
a stone you can't get around.
But the stone is me! If you're looking for me,
you'll find me on the way, not in the way."

**Romans 9:33**

# CONTENTS

PROLOGUE

# SPECIAL DELIVERY

The doorbell startled me. It was 9:15 p.m. *It's too late for a delivery*, I thought, *and it's an unusual hour for unexpected company.* Turning on the porch light provided no help in solving the mystery. No one was visible as I peered through the glass pane in the front door.

"Gene," I called, "did *you* hear the doorbell ring?"

"Yes," he shouted from his office. "Who's there?"

Gene joined me as I unlocked the door. There wasn't a car in sight, and no one appeared to be anywhere near our home. Suddenly my eyes were drawn to a package next to the door. It glistened as the yard lights reflected off metallic ribbon and gilded holiday wrapping paper.

*Where did it come from? How was it delivered? What was inside?* The size and grandeur of the package made the mystery surrounding the delivery all the more intriguing. It *was* two weeks before Christmas, but I couldn't imagine who would have dropped off the gift. Picking it up, I stepped back inside the front door and noticed a card on top of the gift. It simply read: *Mom.*

Now I was certain the package had been delivered to the wrong house. My only child was in prison. Was this a cruel joke? At best, it must be a mistake.

Gene and I looked at each other, bewildered. Neither of us spoke. Curiosity was getting the best of me. After all, the package was left on *my* porch. And I *am* a mom. Certainly no one could fault me for opening the package.

Sensing my hesitancy, Gene nodded, and I opened the card. Much

13

to my shock, the note inside appeared to be in the handwriting of my son, who was incarcerated at Hardee Correctional Institution, forty miles away. I could feel tears forming in my eyes as Gene and I read the message:

> *Dear Mom,*
>
> *It's been nine years since I was able to be home with you and Dad for Christmas. I miss you so much! You have poured love and encouragement into my life, and you have supplied me with so many educational and ministry tools to help my fellow inmates here at the prison. You and Dad always keep enough money in my account so I can purchase personal hygiene items and additional food items so I feel like a human being who still has somebody who loves me in the middle of a maximum security prison.*
>
> *I wanted to do something special for you this year. I hope you enjoy the gift. It would bring me lots of joy if it's something you like. I hope every time you wear it you think of how much you mean to me.*
>
> *Love,*
>
> *J.P.*

Tears spilled down my cheeks as I began opening the exquisite package, so carefully wrapped with tender loving care. I knew it would have been impossible for my son to wrap and send this package on his own — the prison would never allow it. But who helped him to make this clandestine delivery? And what about the note that looked like it was penned in his handwriting?

Lifting the lid off the large gift box, I discovered mounds of tissue paper covering the surprise. As the paper fell to the floor, there it was: the most gorgeous russet-colored silk jacket I had ever laid eyes on — a perfect match for my red hair. Slipping it on, I headed for the full-length mirror in our bedroom. It was just the right size — as if a tailor had custom-measured me for a flawless fit. The quality was better than I could have afforded for myself that Christmas, and inside the package was a matching scarf to make the ensemble complete.

I clung to the note, still amazed that someone could have pulled off this coup without my knowledge. I felt as if God had kissed me on the forehead and said:

*Carol, I know where your son is and how much you long to have him at home with you. I know your heart hurts. I love your son even more than you do. I have not forgotten him, and I have not forgotten you. Your family Christmases will not be the way you once dreamed they would be, but I want you to be encouraged. I love you with an everlasting love, and I won't ever walk away from you. I am comforting your son as you are opening this package. Merry Christmas, my child. Remember, I am close to the brokenhearted.*

That night I discovered something new about God and something I had forgotten about myself. He loves to interject divine surprises into our lives — and I still had the childlike wonder to appreciate them. His timing is always perfect, but it had been a while since I had been surprised by joy, wonder, and grace in the middle of one of the tight spots of life.

The mystery of the clandestine delivery lasted several days before I discovered that my friend Pam had exchanged letters with my son and arranged for this gift to be delivered on his behalf. Before making the stealthy trip to my front porch, Pam checked my schedule to be sure I would be home, and her daughter, Kirstie, placed the gift outside the door. I was surprised to find out that Kirstie, with Pam's help, had penned the note, based on what they believed would best express J.P.'s thoughts. Kirstie's handwriting was a dead ringer for his. The note was like an extra bow on the gift of the reassurance of being loved by my son and cared for by God. It was a divine surprise. A holy hug. A sweet taste of grace in a hard place.

That's what this book is about — finding "the grace place" when you feel as if life's circumstances have placed you in a tight spot: between a rock and a hard place.

You may have read about our family's experience with our "hard place" in *When I Lay My Isaac Down* or in *A New Kind of Normal*. If not, let me fill you in with the speed version. I'll fast-forward to the birth of our only child, Jason Paul Kent (we call him J.P.), because in order to grasp the full weight of our story, you need to understand the bond within our family of three.

J.P.'s birth was a delightful surprise — not that I was having a baby, but that he was a boy! I didn't know the gender of my child before I gave birth, so when the doctor announced, "It's a boy!" I had the joy of watching sheer delight spread immediately over my husband's face. Gene had a son, and he could hardly contain himself. Little did I know then that becoming a mother would ultimately be the hardest, most heart-stopping, emotionally charged, and gut-wrenching assignment of my life.

Our son grew up happy. His teachers praised him. His grandpa took him on fishing trips. He and his dad began running together and eventually participated in a half marathon. Jason was focused, disciplined, compassionate, and lots of fun! He always kept a to-do list. He listed his goals and marked off his accomplishments. He had a strong faith, and as he matured he developed a determined mind-set to change the world for the better through military or political leadership.

After receiving an appointment to the U.S. Naval Academy, he continued his commitment to mental, academic, physical, and spiritual disciplines. Following the rigors of "plebe summer," we enjoyed four years of traveling to Annapolis for parent weekends. The pride and glory days of color parades, awards ceremonies, clam chowder at The Chart House, and old-fashioned milkshakes at Chick & Ruth's Delly to celebrate our son's small and large accomplishments provided many scrapbook-worthy photographs. Memories to last a lifetime, with many more to come. Until disaster struck — and life changed forever.

Jason's first assignment as a young ensign was nuclear engineering school in Orlando, Florida. He met the girl of his dreams in a local church and fell deliriously, head over heels in love! When Jason's orders changed and he had to be at Surface Warfare Officers School in Newport, Rhode Island, in early September, they decided to get married. Our soon-to-be daughter-in-law had two adorable little girls from a previous marriage, and the day we became in-laws we also became Grampy Gene and Grammy Carol to a three-year-old and a six-year-old whose big brown eyes and precocious personalities quickly stole our hearts.

At the time of our daughter-in-law's divorce, a judge had granted the girls' biological father only supervised visitation with his daughters due to allegations of abuse. During the first year Jason and his new bride were married, the girls' father petitioned the court for unsupervised visitation. It appeared that he was going to get it. J.P. began to unravel emotionally, mentally, and spiritually as his anxiety mounted over the safety of his stepdaughters.

Just over a year after our son's marriage, we received a middle-of-the night phone call that shocked and horrified us. Our son had been arrested for the murder of his wife's first husband. For several moments, we couldn't breathe. Waves of nausea combined with disbelief immobilized us. Our minds whirled.

*This is a bad dream. We'll wake up soon, and life will be normal.*

*Our son is not capable of murder.*

*If God loves us, how could he allow this to happen?*

*I'm going to be sick again.*

But the news from the caller was true. Jason had pulled a trigger in a public parking lot. A man died. Another family — a father, stepmother, fiancée, and sister — were planning a funeral for the man our son had killed. We experienced another round of sickness and grief as we considered what the family of the victim was experiencing. There could be no do-overs. No opportunity to fix what had happened. A man was dead. Jason had been arrested for killing him. It was the kind of shock no parent ever wants to get.

We went through two and a half years and seven postponements of Jason's trial for first-degree murder. Ultimately he was convicted and sentenced in a Florida state courtroom to life in prison without the possibility of parole. Our requests for evidentiary hearings and appeals have been exhausted at both the state and federal levels. We are living daily between a rock and a hard place. Humanly speaking, we can't see any possibility that our son, who was twenty-five years old at the time of his arrest, will walk in freedom in this lifetime.

I now believe it is possible to die from a broken heart. I have experienced the agony of crying until I have no more tears. I know the sadness of watching hopes and dreams for my son die. I have watched what happens to many inmates who, when all hope is taken away, find no internal motivation to act responsibly. There is no reason to learn, to grow, to contribute positively to someone else's life. I have watched the eyes of "lifers" lose their sparkle and become empty. A life sentence is a walking death for many. A different kind of punishment than the death chamber. It is the death of hope.

So why am I writing this book? Because I passionately believe, through personal experience, that when we reach the absolute end of our ability to move in a forward direction because the rock in the middle of our path is immovable, there is a better option than giving in to resignation or despair. When we are stuck between a rock and a hard place, we have not reached the end of the road.

One day when I was struggling with "sad mama" thoughts, my sister Jennie e-mailed me a verse from the Bible that captivated my heart. Even though I grew up as a preacher's kid, went to church almost every Sunday, and have read and studied the Bible throughout my life, I didn't recall hearing Romans 9:33. When Jennie shared Eugene Peterson's rendering from *The Message*, the verse came alive for me:

> "Careful! I've put a huge stone on the road to Mount Zion,
>> a stone you can't get around.
> But the stone is me! If you're looking for me,
>> you'll find me on the way, not in the way."

It has now been more than a decade ago, right in the middle of my life, that I ran into a huge boulder — the likes of which I had never encountered on my lifelong walk with God. It could have been my stopping place — the point at which I lost not only some of my most cherished dreams but also my faith, my joy, my purpose, and my passion to go on. Instead, I found out that the Rock in my path represented not an obstacle but an opportunity to encounter the living God in surprising, sometimes astonishing ways. As I have learned to press into the Rock in the middle of my hard places, I have discovered that I am actually in a position of safety, refuge, and grace. Year after year, God continues to transform my hard places into grace places where I discover surprising gifts of faith, mercy, contentment, praise, blessing, freedom, laughter, and adventure — tailor-made for me with his tender, loving care.

You probably picked up this book because you feel caught in one of those tight spots of life where the experience you are facing is difficult, if not unbearable. I pray that you will come to realize that the pain of being in this place need not cause you to lose hope. On the contrary, being "stuck" between a rock and a hard place can lead to a transforming and liberating encounter with the only true Rock — God himself. If you press into the Rock instead of trying to get around it, you will discover a surprise far better than a Christmas gift specially delivered to your doorstep. On the road that is your life right now, you can find a new way of thinking about your circumstances, as well as an astonishing experience of grace, tailor-made just for you. As you encounter God "on" the way, not "in" the way, you may come to know him as you never have before.

CHAPTER 1

# GRACE IN THE HARDEST OF PLACES

## SURPRISED BY FAITH

I know God will not give me anything I can't handle.
I just wish he didn't trust me so much.
**Mother Teresa**

My heart was doing cartwheels in my chest. I was sure I must be having a heart attack. First I took long, deliberate breaths. Then I coughed hard, thinking that would jolt the fist-sized pump inside my chest into functioning properly. It was the week before our son's trial for first-degree murder. Even though he had already been given seven other trial dates, followed by seven postponements, I thought, *It's really going to take place this time.*

Gene and I were tired — bone tired. Tired of waiting to know what the future held for our only child and tired of the stress and constant anxiety. There were days when I wished I could go to sleep and not wake up. I was weary from being an advocate for my son at the county jail as he awaited a trial date, and I was sick of responding to questions from reporters, acquaintances, and especially from nosey individuals who wanted information they could share with other people.

I had not taken a break from speaking following Jason's arrest —

not because I was deeply spiritual, but because working hard helped to numb the pain, and ministry was our livelihood, the only way we could pay for our son's attorney. But we had been warned not to speak publicly about what had happened until after the trial. I had been saying out loud, "God, you are good! You are trustworthy!" But was I saying those things because they were programmed into me by my family and my ministry background, or because I really believed them?

Thirty months after our son's arrest in Florida, his trial began, and five days later, he was convicted and sentenced for first-degree murder. We returned home to Michigan weighed down with fear for our son's safety in prison, apprehensive about the future for his family and ours, uncertain about how to begin the appeal process, incredulous that we could be living a story that was so foreign to our former life, shocked that our prayers seemed useless, and overwhelmed by questions we couldn't answer. How could we encourage our son from so far away? How could we give tangible support to his wife and two young stepdaughters? Now that I could speak from a public platform about the trial, could I tell such an intense story without falling apart? I had always prided myself on not being one of those "overly emotional" speakers.

Instead of getting better after the trial, the wild heartbeats and calisthenics in my chest got worse. Even when I tried to rest, there was something wrong. Sleep was elusive, and I couldn't deny that my heart was skipping beats or, at the least, beating in an abnormal way. At Gene's insistence, I made an appointment with a cardiologist to find out if my heart was malfunctioning. My father had already had two bypass surgeries, so perhaps the real culprit was genetic. Following an EKG and a stress test, I prepared myself for what was sure to be bad news from the specialist.

On the day of the follow-up appointment, the nurse led me to a private room where Gene and I waited for the doctor. When he sat down with us, he said, "Carol, the test results have come back, and I have good news for you. Your heart is fine." I felt relief, coupled with confusion. *Then what is wrong with me?* I wondered. I could feel my heart beating erratically even as I sat before the cardiologist, having received a clean bill of health. The physician continued. "I know you are going through a lot right now. The symptoms you have been experiencing are not uncommon in people who are under this much stress. Based on a thorough evaluation of your physical health and an understanding of how the human body can respond to stress, I can conclude that you are suffering from severe panic attacks."

I was flabbergasted by the report. How was it possible that my anxiety was so out of control? Didn't I trust God enough? Wasn't I clinging to the biblical truths I'd known from my earliest years in Sunday school? I had memorized many of the "fear not ..." Scripture verses, and I had not given up on my faith, even after Jason's conviction. Or had I? Was my faith as strong as I thought it was? Did I still feel sure that God loved me and that he was working things out for my good and for the good of my family members? Did I believe God was just and kind? Or were these foundational convictions slowly disintegrating? My son was not a threat to society at large. He had acted out of overwhelming fear for his stepdaughters' safety. I did not believe he was in his "right mind" in the days and weeks leading up to his devastating actions. That didn't justify my son's crime, but if God knew Jason's true heart, why didn't he intervene in the legal process so that Jason's sentence would one day allow him to walk in freedom? Did God really care about any of us?

## Questions of Faith and Conviction

In the years since Jason's arrest and conviction, I have heard from many people with faith questions of their own.

✢ ✢ ✢

I have a broken heart and shattered dreams. My only child was killed in an automobile accident last spring. Where was God?

✢ ✢ ✢

My autistic son is driving me crazy and ruining my marriage. I love him so much, but I don't know how we can deal with him anymore. I am losing my ability to cope. Why did God allow my child to be born with this condition?

✤ ✤ ✤

My husband gave me a sexually transmitted disease while denying he has been involved in an ongoing affair with a woman who works in his office. He maintained his innocence until I caught him in the act. He says he loves me and doesn't want to lose our family. He must think I'm an idiot. Does God expect me to forgive my husband and stay married to him?

✤ ✤ ✤

When I was sixteen I had an abortion. For the past twelve years I have been dragging around invisible chains of shame and guilt. I've asked for God's forgiveness, but I still feel like a murderer. Why don't I have enough faith to believe that I can really be set free from my wrong choices in the past?

✤ ✤ ✤

We raised our son in a Christian home, but he is drunk and high more than he is clean and sober. We have exhausted our savings accounts with the cost of treatment centers. Every time he gets involved in a recovery program he's OK for a short while, and then we go through the entire ordeal all over again. My child was raised in the church, and he always got excellent grades. We did a good job of parenting him, but his choices are always destructive. Why do some alcoholics and addicts get well while others don't? Why won't God heal our child?

✤ ✤ ✤

My older sister, my mother, and her mother are all breast cancer survivors. Because of our family history, I made the wrenching decision to have a prophylactic double mastectomy three years ago. I just found out that I have ovarian cancer. My prognosis is not good. I am only thirty-four years old, and I have two daughters. My entire family is praying for my healing, but we are devastated. I don't know what to think anymore about trusting God, much less what to tell my girls. I'm afraid that if I don't make it, they will lose not only their mother but their faith as well.

✤ ✤ ✤

My mother was brutally raped and killed by a man who was strung out on drugs. She was only thirty-eight years old, and I was only thirteen when I lost her. Her murderer just wrote a letter to me, asking for forgiveness. I am a Christian, but I don't know if I am capable of responding to this man and granting his request. I feel so bitter.

## Stuck between a Rock and a Hard Place

Since I've been writing and speaking about our journey with our son, Gene and I have received hundreds of letters from people who find themselves up against impassable obstacles. Something has happened to them or to their loved ones that is painful, shameful, or life altering — and sometimes unfair, cruel, or previously unimaginable. One day life is normal and full of promise, and the next day the phone rings, or the accident happens, or the deceit is uncovered, or the mental breakdown occurs, or the police officer knocks on the door, or the doctor shakes his head as he walks out of the operating room — and the comfortable, happy, and "normal" life you were leading is abruptly interrupted or completely derailed.

You have been stopped in your tracks. You are up against a rock in the path of your life that appears gigantic in its magnitude. You can't get around it. You can't get through it. You can't negotiate your way to a more favorable result. The damage has been done. The lies have been revealed. The disease has wrecked havoc. The baby cannot be placed back in the womb. The accident report cannot be rewritten. The clock cannot be turned back. The shame or guilt is unbearable. The losses are staggering. Your faith has been tested. You are questioning long-held beliefs about the goodness and mercy of God. You are stuck between a rock and a place that feels very hard indeed.

After my son was arrested for murder, I was deeply perplexed over what had gone on in his mind prior to his crime. Gene and I were involved parents who knew we had raised our child to know right from wrong. Throughout Jason's growing-up years, we watched him make mostly good choices. He never got into fights at school and didn't get caught up in the drug culture during a time when many of our friends were dealing with unexpected and sometimes unlawful behavior by

25

their children. Jason was a peacemaker, not a violent person. We felt blessed, and we were optimistic about his future. He cared about making a positive difference in the lives of others and had compassion for people who were abused and mistreated. Our son wasn't perfect, but he was heading in a positive direction, and we were proud of him. What possibly could have led him to believe he was so "stuck" in the middle of a crisis that he had no choice but to take matters into his own hands?

In one of his letters to us, written several years after his arrest, he explains some of the erosion of his thought process. In retrospect, he sees clearly that he responded to a daunting challenge with fearful desperation rooted in self-reliance. "In short," he told us, "the reason I am in prison today for killing a man is that I trusted in myself and doubted God."

*Dear Mom and Dad,*

*As I write now, almost ten years removed from the horrific day my mind snapped, it is almost impossible to recall exactly what led up to my devastating actions. I do remember the intensity of my emotional angst as my ability to protect my beloved stepdaughters appeared to be slipping away. My wife and I had sought legal counsel from an experienced and highly recommended lawyer, and I had tried man-to-man reasoning with the girls' father ... but nothing we did to protect them from what I believed was an imminent threat to their safety appeared to be working. I was becoming demoralized, indignant, and full of fear.*

*I wanted to believe that God cared about our lives and our problems and that I could trust him, but I couldn't see any evidence of this. Over and over in my mind I imagined my daughters coming to me in the future, sobbing out the question: "Daddy, couldn't you have done anything to protect us?" In my determination not to abandon my little girls, I was losing my grip on reality and my ability to reason.*

*As part of the volunteer military, I was willing to stand in harm's*

*way on behalf of my country. As a Christian, I wanted to protect people who couldn't defend themselves. While I was still a student at the U.S. Naval Academy, I had to decide if I was willing to lay down my life, if necessary, to protect American citizens. I knew I could. No father would hesitate to sacrifice his life for his children, and I was no different. Now a battle was raging within me between my faith in God and what I felt I had to do to protect my girls. As my dear friend and fellow inmate, Leon, puts it, "I was relying on my faith in God instead of relying on God for my faith."*

*I would brood on our family's situation while I was at work, and when I came home, I would play with the girls, ride bikes together, wrestle, have dinner, and portray myself as normal. But during any idle moment, my mind would fixate on the topic of protecting my little lambs. When they looked at me with such love, hope, and trust, I felt so proud and privileged to be in their lives. I hadn't had the privilege of seeing them come into this world, but I had been entrusted with the honor of cherishing and providing for them. I had such a strong desire to love them with wisdom and strength and to protect them from bad guys, burglars, and the boogeyman. I was so afraid of betraying their trust in me.*

*During this time I'd wake up at night and feel I was a failure as a father in my duty to provide safety and security for my family. I lost more and more sleep and became exhausted and fixated on my fear. As my trust in God eroded, I became more and more restless and angry and frustrated, and by the time my hope died completely, I was left with only my love for my daughters and my fear for their safety. I was like a man possessed.*

*All of this built up over ten months, and I slowly entered into a deep depression. I was skilled at hiding how I felt most of the time. Compartmentalizing your life, particularly for security purposes, is a tactic often employed in the military, especially in Special Forces. My habit of not telling anyone everything carried over to the problem I was facing in my personal life, so even though my wife saw* some of my angst and the chinks in my emotional armor, I wouldn't elaborate on my pain. If I had opened up my heart and had the humility to be transparent, then maybe my spouse or a friend or fellow soldier would have been able to help me make a wise decision instead of a reckless and destructive one.

As my mind deteriorated, I operated with a form of tunnel vision. I came to the conclusion that the only recourse was to rely on myself and my military training to eradicate a clear and present threat. The weekend of the murder, it was like I was watching a movie, with myself as just one of the characters on the screen. When I opened the door to my vehicle to drive to the city where my stepdaughters' father lived, I went on autopilot—like I was jumping off the back ramp of a C-130 in a parachute. I didn't think; I simply performed what I'd been trained to do. When you're falling through the air, looking back up at the aircraft while it's flying away, there is no getting back inside. Likewise, after I opened the door of my vehicle, it was as though I was on a mission and had my orders. I'd done plenty of difficult military work already and knew how to just buckle down and drive forward. "You don't have to like it," I thought. "You just have to do it."

After my arrest I felt numb, almost like I was in a dream. I was left in an interrogation cell for several hours and then transported to the county jail where I was fingerprinted and stripped. My head was shaved, and I was confined. It was like watching my life from outside my body. At first I couldn't grasp where my delusional thinking had led me.

As I slowly reconnected with reality, the immensity of it all—including the harm I had inadvertently done to those I had sought to protect—began to sink in. I was completely empty, exhausted, and depressed, and I felt like a failure as a man, as a husband, as a father, as a son, and as a Christian. I considered the massive shame for you, Mom and Dad, as I destroyed our family name, and I envisioned the horror that you, along with my wife and *stepdaughters, would experience as you were dragged with me through the trial. I had no idea at that time just how much pain I would put all of you through. And I certainly had not considered the huge loss and sorrow of my victim's family. I know I have caused you so much agony, Mom and Dad. I can only imagine the pain I have caused the father of the man I killed. I have stolen from him his relationship with his son.*

*Only in retrospect can I recognize how arrogant, self-righteous, and self-reliant I became in the weeks leading up to the murder as my fears and worries consumed me. My lack of trust in God to intervene on behalf of my family left me feeling like I was the only one who could rescue them. I still believed that God existed and he'd sent Jesus to secure our eternity through his sacrifice, but I didn't believe he would come through in the present. I lived out a practical atheism in many ways because I didn't really expect God to act—or maybe even to care. I trusted and counted on myself. I relied on my efforts, my skills, my weakened and worry-filled mind to get me and my family through. My lack of faith in God led me to take action that did the opposite. I had experienced a crisis of faith, and I had not behaved as a strong Christian man in the face of it. Instead, my actions had reaped death, devastation, grief, and destruction of everything my life had previously represented.*

*Now I see so clearly that my sins make me in dire need of a Savior, and I can never "make it" on my own. I don't ever need any less grace than anyone else. My arrogant pride and self-righteousness allowed me to embrace Christ for eternity in heaven, but I had little trust in him for the here and now. I now know to my core that I not only can't make it into heaven without him; I can't make it tomorrow or the next day or even the next five minutes. If God doesn't show up in and through my life, I am undone. I cannot be the man I want to be—or God wants me to be—via self-effort. My drive alone will never get me to the destination. I need him continually ...*

The Bible states that "faith is being sure of what we hope for and certain of what we do not see."[1] It means putting all our hopes, dreams, and fears into the hands of God, even though we have no way of knowing how a personal challenge will turn out. It is relinquishing control of the outcome of whatever concerns us.

When the obstacle in our path is monstrous in size or character, choosing faith in what we do not see can feel risky and unnatural — even opposed to common sense. My son says that he could not see choosing this kind of faith as an option by the time he committed his crime. He was driven by his obsessive fear. But, as the woman whose story you're about to read discovered, choosing to trust God instead of oneself can be the wisest, most liberating, and most important decision of our lives.

## Crazy! — Claudine's Story

I slammed the phone down, covered my ears, and screamed at the top of my lungs, "I'm going to hell!"

My son was two years old. My husband had spent the past year training for a new job in another city, often working eighty hours a week. And I was going crazy!

I had noticed the emotional changes in me shortly after our son was born. I knew it wasn't uncommon for new mothers to go through a period of anxiety and depression after childbirth, so I chalked up my experience to the "baby blues" and waited for the emotions to pass.

Instead, they got worse. I couldn't seem to accomplish anything. As a woman who had always been strong and capable of multitasking, I was now a broken, lost, fearful, and weepy mess. The simplest tasks, like washing dishes, picking up a to-go cup left over from lunch, doing laundry, or even carrying my son's diaper to the trash, became practically impossible. It was so bad that my mother's first action upon entering my home would be to grab a trash bag and begin picking up the mess.

I was tired all the time, but couldn't sleep. I was sad, yet had a beautiful blue-eyed boy to make me laugh. I was afraid of what was happening to me, but too afraid to tell anyone. I cried constantly, apologized for everything, and was convinced I was losing my mind.

I was fighting physical illness as well. If it wasn't bronchitis, it was strep throat, or a urinary tract infection, or a skin rash. I was chronically ill. And none of the doctors I went to could tell me what was wrong. I was on antibiotics weekly. It seemed that one infection would leave only to be replaced by another. I was completely run-down — in body, mind, and spirit.

Frightened, I finally sought help at a well-known medical clinic in a nearby city. I was put through the paces of a thorough physical, complete with multiple diagnostic procedures for virtually every major organ in my body. The medical experts' conclusion: "You're healthy as a horse." They couldn't find anything significantly wrong with me.

Now I really knew I was crazy. I shouldn't be sick. And everyone else would be better off without me.

For the rest of that week, I planned how to run away. I believed that if I could leave for a few months, just disappear where no one could find me, I could somehow heal my weary body and mind. So I plotted. When to leave (the next week), where to go (to a resort area with lots of people so I'd blend in), how to tell my family that I was OK but convince them not to look for me (through my good friend, Suzanne), how to get there (this was hardest because I didn't want to leave a trail), what work to do (housekeeping at a hotel — certainly the last place anyone would look), how to hide (by talking to no one). As the week went on, all these thoughts and plans became real. I was going to do it. I knew beyond a shadow of a doubt that my husband and son would be better off after I was away from them.

The day I screamed at the top of my lungs was a turning point. It started out like every other day: play with my son, read books, run a few errands. As usual, I hadn't slept much the night before, so when nap time came I was eager to get Logan down for a snooze.

Logan, however, had a different idea. That day, no matter what I did, he would not lie down. Lying on his back on my bed, he stuck his little feet up for me to pull his socks off. Hooking my finger in the socks I began to pull ... at the same time he began to kick. He was just playing. But I snapped. Yanking him up by the socks, I held him upside down, over the bed, and began to shake him, screaming, "YOU HAVE GOT TO TAKE A NAP. MOMMY NEEDS A NAP!"

I only shook him for a moment, but I was so out of control I terrified myself. He was still screaming as I eased him back down to the bed. Lying down beside him I wept, saying over and over, "Mommy's sorry. Mommy's sorry." I had never done anything like that before. I never wanted to again.

Frantically, I called my father-in-law and said, "Someone had better come and get this kid before I hurt him." Ten minutes later, Papa Bob showed up in his green truck to take Logan for the day.

I stood there and watched them drive away. Tears were streaming down my face. Everyone said there was nothing wrong. It was all in my head. But I knew that something was desperately wrong. I just didn't know how to fix it.

I picked up the phone and called my mom. She wasn't home. I called Dad's office. Not there. I called my friend Suzanne. Not home. I wanted to find someone ... anyone ... to pray for me. I dialed more than a dozen numbers and got only answering machines or busy signals. I was all alone.

That's when I slammed down the phone and screamed. I didn't just think I was going to hell; I thought I was already there.

I lay down on the bed, curled up into a ball, and sobbed. "I can't take any more, God. What is wrong with me? I go to church three times a week. I do all the things I'm supposed to do. Why are you letting all this happen? *Why don't you do something*?!"

It seemed like I had lain there all day, but it was probably just a few hours. I felt completely immobilized. I no longer had the momentum to carry out my plan to run away, yet I could see no path forward. I was stuck — flattened between an immovable obstacle and the hardest place I had ever been in my life. The enemy was whispering in my ear that I could not be well, that I would never be better. The obstacle was my illness — whatever it was — and the hard place was my intractable despair. Or so I thought. But God was reminding me that even in this crushing, airless space, he was with me. In fact, he was right in front of me. It was as if he was saying, "Claudine, if you really want to get better, you need to press even harder into me."

I found myself praying out loud, "Lord, I don't understand this at all. I hate it." I didn't expect what came out of my mouth next: "But if it never changes, if I'm really crazy, if I stay sick, if no one ever understands, *I will still praise you!*"

Even though I could see no way out, God's grace began to pour through the cracks of my self-reliance and illuminate my thinking. I realized that I couldn't fix what was wrong with me. But I could change what I believed about it. I had a choice to make.

"Lord," I continued, "you are the only certain thing in my life. No matter what happens, I will choose to praise you. Right now I choose to trust you with my family and with my future. But God, I don't believe this is your will for my life ... for our lives. I refuse to give up hope. I refuse to believe that this is your final answer and that this is what you want my life to look like. I'm going to hold on to my faith in your ability to redeem and restore. I'm going to choose to believe that somehow, someway, I will get better."

Now, I'd like to tell you that everything turned around fast. It didn't. But I had made a decision. I chose to trust God no matter what the outcome and to believe in his goodness despite how I felt. I had to remind myself often that it was a choice to hold on to faith. It was not an emotion. On most days I didn't feel any different. I still cried — a lot. Sometimes I still thought about running away. But the decision I made that painful day changed my life forever. When I chose to stop focusing on how lousy I felt, I opened my mind to trusting that I could be healed.

Over time, I learned that part of getting well and staying well would include being proactive in making my life better, one action step at a time. Whenever I felt particularly down, I practiced acting as if I really believed that God was in the process of restoring me. If that meant getting out of bed when I didn't feel like it, washing a pile of dirty dishes, picking up the clutter, and carrying out the trash, then that's what I did. Some days, taking even a simple action was far from easy. Sometimes if I got just one thing done I called it a good day. If I got two done it was a *really* good day. What mattered was making the choice to cooperate with God in tangible ways rather than simply fighting against my moods or my circumstances.

As I lived out my decision to relinquish my future at the same time I was choosing hope, God began to show me a way out of my hell, and he taught me something that profoundly changed the way I respond to suffering: If I choose to *look for God* right in the midst of my circumstances rather than looking for *a way out* of my hard place, he will reveal himself to me. More often than not, the very thing that is bringing me so much anguish is what God wants to use to show me more of his character, his faithfulness, and his plan for my life.

Back when I was suffering from what I now know was postpartum depression, mental illness wasn't talked about in my circles, and clinical depression wasn't nearly as well understood as it is today. The doctors who told me that there was nothing wrong with me simply didn't look in the right direction. I initially did not get the medical help I needed. But God did not leave me hopeless. When I had exhausted every human resource I knew, he shone his light into the blackness of my hard place. He brought to my mind the psalmist's words, which have now become my life verse: "But as for me, I will always have hope; I will praise you more and more."[2] By learning how to exercise my freedom to choose hope over despair, my mind became a training ground for faith.

Slowly, I got better. I stopped planning my escape from reality and learned to face my emotions with courage, grounded in my choice to believe that God would be gracious to me when I found myself between a rock and a hard place again.

My son is twenty-one now, and I never again had to call someone to save him from my out-of-control behavior. I still struggle with depression sometimes, but I don't panic over it. Instead, I make the choice to reflect on what I have learned and on whom I can trust:

> I remember my affliction and my wandering,
>> the bitterness and the gall.
>
> I well remember them,
>> and my soul is downcast within me.
>
> Yet this I call to mind
>> and therefore I have hope:
>
> Because of the LORD's great love we are not consumed,
>> for his compassions never fail.
>
> They are new every morning;
>> great is your faithfulness.[3]

I keep choosing to praise him more and more. And then I go wash the dishes.[4]

## Enough Already!

When Claudine and I first met, I was impressed by her bright smile and her upbeat and engaging demeanor. I never imagined the inner chaos she had been living with that rocked her to the core of her being and challenged her faith. Since then, I have met countless people who have shared with me their experiences of being all but crushed between a rock and a hard place, and I have come to deeply appreciate the way Scripture speaks to the kind of suffering that can shake our faith and threaten to turn it to rubble.

As a young adult who was trying to live out her purpose and working diligently to do things that mattered with her life, I read the Bible on a regular basis. However, there was one book in that lengthy compilation of sixty-six that I skimmed over rather than reading carefully. It was the book of Job. I had a basic understanding that Job was a man who diligently tried to do what was right. He obeyed God and used his vast resources to bless his family and others. But his life took a drastic turn that never seemed fair to me — so I preferred skipping that story and sticking with more inspirational passages.

Job had a large family — ten children! At one point he also owned seven thousand sheep, three thousand camels, one thousand cows, and five hundred donkeys. Now, that's a lot of livestock! He also had many servants to help him manage his huge estate.

Then, quite unexpectedly, everything changed. Check out his list of losses:

+ His donkeys were stolen.
+ Most of his faithful servants were killed.
+ Lightning struck his shepherds and his sheep — and they all died.
+ Marauders stole his camels.
+ A fierce storm killed *all ten* of his children.
+ His health disintegrated.
+ Painful, repulsive sores broke out all over his body, and he wound up sitting in a dump where he used a broken piece of pottery to scrape his oozing wounds.

Job's words reveal his plight in living color:

> "If my misery could be weighed,
>     if you could pile the whole bitter load on the scales,
>   it would be heavier than all the sand of the sea!
>     Is it any wonder that I'm screaming like a caged cat?"[5]

If you have ever owned a cat, this mental picture is vivid. Cats don't like to do what they are told, and they often don't come when they are called — but cage one up and see what happens. The sound they make when they are fearful or forced into situations they dislike is a strident wail that assaults human ears.

Job not only experienced unthinkable personal circumstances, but he also had a wife who mocked him. She said, "Still holding on to your precious integrity, are you? Curse God and be done with it!"[6]

I admit that when the Enemy tempts me to fall into a depressed mind-set, one of his tactics is to remind me that I'm a good mother and that Gene and I raised our child to be a man of integrity and right living — but terrible things happened, and our son did not end up with the life we prayed for. The Enemy likes to whisper, "You've honored God and tried to live by biblical principles, but he still didn't keep your son from murdering a man — and now your son will rot in a prison cell for the rest of his life. Why don't you curse God and give up on following him? He didn't come through for you."

Job's response to his wife humbles me: "'You're talking like an empty-headed fool. We take the good days from God — why not also the bad days?' Not once through all this did Job sin. He said nothing against God."[7]

Nevertheless, Job got the ultimate sucker punch. Not only did his closest friends fail to sympathize with his extraordinary trial, but their traditional religious beliefs led them to believe he must have sinned and God was punishing him. Eventually he entered what appears to be a period of serious depression. "But I don't have the strength to endure," he said. "I have nothing to live for."[8]

Depression over ongoing negative circumstances can wear us down until death looks more attractive than life. Job verbalizes intense inner turmoil, along with the physical symptoms that often accompany depression. At one point he said, "I am innocent, but it makes no difference to me — I despise my life."[9] Later he added: "I can hardly see from crying so much; I'm nothing but skin and bones."[10] And, "My days are over. My hopes have disappeared. My heart's desires are broken."[11]

At one time or another, each of us walks through suffering that feels intense, not unlike Job's. The Bible records a positive end to his story: "GOD blessed Job's later life even more than his earlier life. He ended up with fourteen thousand sheep, six thousand camels, one thousand teams of oxen, and one thousand donkeys."[12] He had more children and enjoyed four generations of offspring until he died at a ripe old age — which reminds all of us that there *can* be life after depression and overwhelmingly difficult experiences. Things are not always as bleak as they appear when we are stuck between a rock and a hard place.

## A Stranger's Question

As Gene and I continue to live out a life far different from what we dreamed of when we were younger, we have encountered a variety of responses from people. One Sunday morning we had just shared our story during services at a church near Toronto. While we were standing in the lobby, a man walked up, shook Gene's hand, and asked, "Did you ever lose your faith in God while going through the arrest, trial, and conviction of your son? Or even during the past few years, when you prayed for a miracle and saw nothing positive happen?"

We have been asked this question many times since J.P.'s arrest, and we have both thought a lot about our relationship with God. Recently, Gene journaled about his experience with faith during the most challenging journey of our lives.

> Soon after the murder, while our son was in a cell in the Orange County Jail, I believed that God knew and cared about our circumstances. He was deeply grieved over our son's actions on October 24, 1999, and he did not cause any of the events to take place. But looking back, I think I was expecting God to do something miraculous by allowing my son to one day walk in freedom. I certainly couldn't get my mind around what a life sentence really meant.
>
> After Jason was sentenced, I realized God was not allowing a miracle to take place immediately or in the foreseeable future. Was I mad at God? Did I question his goodness? In retrospect I can say I was not so much mad at God as I was "hurt" by what he had allowed—not just for my son, but for the victim as well. I believed an all-knowing God could have stopped this crime from happening. But he didn't. In my heart I knew God had the ability and desire to use these horrible events for good. He is amazingly creative in his

ability to accomplish unexpected positive resolutions. But it is still hard for me to see "the good."

No, I have not lost my faith in God over everything that has happened with my son. It sometimes seems that people expect me to lose my faith, as if Christianity only works when life is smooth, happy, and void of significant obstacles. But as I observe life — for myself and for others — I see that it is usually hard. It contains momentary times of joy, but it is often full of uncomfortable circumstances, grave consequences for human sin, and overwhelming sorrow. My faith shows me that God himself had to live with sorrow, and that provides an example for me. As a Father, he lost his Son, but he used that loss for ultimate good.

I weep for the father who lost his son at the hands of my son. But I hold on to faith that even on the days when I can't see any redemption, God is working in this situation. He will not waste the enormous grief and pain of two earthly fathers who lost their sons in such different ways.

Gene and I continue to learn that faith is not simply a belief we embrace with our intellect; it is a living, breathing approach to whatever is in front of us in the here and now. Faith must have "feet" on it, and developing a faith that works in the hard places of life requires practice. For us, that means choosing to get up every morning and put one foot in front of the other, trusting that God is still at work in our situation.

On some days I see what God is doing and celebrate that, even though Jason Kent still resides in a maximum security prison, some very good things are happening. On other days I have no visible proof that there is any positive momentum in the midst of a bleak situation. I feel very "stuck" at those times. And yes, I still have anxiety attacks occasionally. But on my worst days I have the best opportunities to practice the kind of faith that relies on God alone.

## The Ultimate Gift

When my sister pointed out Romans 9:33 to me — the "stone on the road" that can become a stumbling block — I was so intrigued that I had to do some research. How had I missed this gem in the center of a well-known Scripture passage? The verse falls right in the middle of a long treatise on the subject of salvation coming to us through simple faith, not by our good deeds. This can be a tough concept for those of us who would like our virtuous behavior to count toward extra credit with God. We like to think that if we behave charitably and try hard to please God, we will be rewarded with a life that just gets better and better. But this is exactly the error in thinking that the apostle Paul, quoting the prophet Isaiah, is warning against in this part of his letter to the Romans. When we trust in our own "best efforts," we devote ourselves, not necessarily to God, but to mental, academic, physical, and spiritual disciplines that give us a false sense of control — and even a sense of righteousness that may be anything but godly. Even those of us who are sincerely trying to be good Christians can get caught up in "following the rules" and miss the whole point of grace. Instead of throwing ourselves on the mercy of the Rock, we keep trying to earn God's favor — and in this way we "stumble" over the very thing meant to save us from ourselves.

The liberating truth is this: When we are caught between a rock and a hard place, we are given the chance to see our human limitations and our desperate need of divine intervention. Then we are given a choice: Will we place ourselves in a posture of humility and complete dependence on God, or will we just "try harder" and stumble over what could be a transforming encounter with grace?

My son has written me many letters about what he has learned as a convicted murderer who will never walk in freedom apart from a miracle. Nearly eleven years of incarceration has enriched his relationship with God, humbled him in a way that has been paradoxically liberating to his spirit, and given him a chance to find purpose by investing his time in living for others. He has told me:

*Mom, I hate prison. But I refuse to waste prison. I choose to believe that God still has a purpose for me in spite of what I have done and the consequences I am living with. I am committed to looking for opportunities to make a positive difference in the lives of the men around me. And my prayer is that these men, if they are eventually released, will never return here. I'm praying they will be good husbands and fathers and productive members of society when they leave this place. If that happens, my time here is not a waste.*

Even as he lives inside a maximum security compound, my son inspires me to press on and make a difference in the world. I am not living the life I dreamed of — and that has been an unpleasant surprise. I still cry more often than I like to admit. But I can honestly say that my life is meaningful, and even satisfying.

Most important, every day is an opportunity to unwrap more of the ultimate gift: God's grace. In my own hardest places I have encountered the kind of grace that enables me to praise God for eyes to see the pain of others, a heart of compassion to respond, and a determination to provide tangible help to those who are caught between a rock and a hard place of their own. I am discovering that God works best through broken people who know they do not have all the answers. He can use people who have exhausted their own resources and finally realize that negotiating the tight spots of life is not something they do by themselves.

As I continue to face hard circumstances I can't fix, I am given a choice: I can allow myself to be broken in pieces by bashing my will against the obstacle I think is in the way ... or by faith I can lean into the Rock and find a place of safety and rest — a grace place that will save me from myself and give me everything I need to move forward on the road.

## EXPLORING YOUR OWN GRACE PLACE

Most of us, at some point in our lives, will encounter a situation that tests our faith and makes us wonder if God is busy elsewhere and has no idea how much we are hurting. You may not have a son in prison, but your own journey has landed you between a rock and a hard place. Life is definitely different than you anticipated, and you're not sure you can cope with the obstacles you face. Answers are not forthcoming, and you may be questioning God's ways or his character. The most important question, however, is: *How will you respond to your circumstances?* Will you withdraw from your friends and family members? Will you "ease" your way out of situations in which you hear people talk about issues of hope and faith? Or will you remain open to divine surprises in the tight spots of your life?

1. All of us have heard people say, "I'm between a rock and a hard place." Have you been there? If so, what does that expression mean to you?

2. Looking back, when did you first encounter a life situation that stopped you in your tracks? What happened, and how did it impact your faith in God?

3. The poet Patrick Overton writes, "When you come to the edge of all the light you have and take the first step into the darkness of the unknown, you must believe one of two things will happen: There will be something solid for you to stand upon, or you will be taught how to fly."[13] Do you agree or disagree with this statement? Why?

4. On a scale of 1 to 10 (with 10 being high), how would you rate your current faith in God? Do you think it's OK to question your faith? Why or why not?

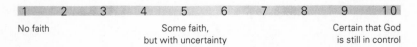

| 1 | 2 | 3 | 4 | 5 | 6 | 7 | 8 | 9 | 10 |

No faith             Some faith,             Certain that God
            but with uncertainty             is still in control

5. Job encountered unthinkable circumstances — livestock stolen or destroyed, servants murdered, children killed, health disintegrated. His wife said, "Curse God and be done with it!"[14] Job's response is shocking in light of his trials. He said, "We take the good days from God — why not also the bad days?"[15] When you encounter a major crisis, is your response more like Job's or like Job's wife, or somewhere in between?

6. Claudine Henry felt like she was going crazy during a clinical depression. She finally admitted she couldn't "fix" what was wrong, but she could choose to praise God in the middle of her circumstances. Rather than trying to find a way out of her hard place, she allowed God to reveal his faithfulness to her. Claudine's story reminds me of something Oswald Chambers said: "Faith is deliberate confidence in the character of God whose ways you may not understand at the time." Sometimes the best place to start rebuilding your faith is by writing out your experience of a difficult impasse that, humanly speaking, seems unfair, unreasonable, and too much to bear. Then write down where you are in your walk with God. Describe what you currently believe about his character and how that impacts your ability to hold on to your faith. If you are in too much pain to take this action step now, that's all right. Simply acknowledging that you're in a painful place and you don't have all the answers is a good place to start. In fact, it can be a humble first step to being surprised by faith in the midst of an unexpected journey.

CHAPTER 2

# Angels in Disguise

## SURPRISED BY MERCY

What did you do today that only
a Christian would have done?
**Corrie ten Boom**

Hailey had been at the home of her grandmother, Penny, for a whole half hour. From the nursery to the living room, Play-Doh, Play-Doh cutters, paper dolls, fairy princess makeup, and princess dresses were strewn everywhere. She announced that she was ready for her bath, and as she pulled out her magic wand that colors her water, she also began pulling off all her clothes as she made her way from the living room to the bathtub.

Arriving in the bathroom, she caught the look on her grandmother's face, which must have conveyed Penny's thoughts about the little girl's path of destruction. Hailey, now in her birthday suit, looked at her grandma and declared: "Oh! Grammy, you really need to work on some MERCY about me!" Then she proceeded with her bath.

While Hailey was contained, Grammy decided to grab a cup of coffee and work on acquiring some mercy!

For some of us, this might be about as much generosity of spirit as we're pressed to dispense on a good day. How easy is that? But the kind of mercy God asks us to extend to others, particularly when they're

45

between a rock and a hard place, sometimes requires us to dig deeply into the soil of spiritual compassion.

## Nurse Betty

It was the first Friday of 2008. I was looking forward to a season of new beginnings. Gene and I spent a nostalgic day boxing up the last of the Christmas decorations and talking about the fun we'd had with the relatives who had traveled from Michigan, Texas, and Georgia to spend time with us and to visit Jason at the prison. Ever since our son's arrest, we had been surrounded with family members during the holidays. It was as if our parents, brothers, sisters, nieces, and nephews instinctively knew how hard it would be for us to be alone at that time of year. And they knew we would not travel out of state and give up the opportunity to visit our son on Christmas Day.

Every room in our home had been packed with people. Both my office and Gene's were transformed into extra bedrooms with the help of an old mattress in one room and a newfangled blow-up makeshift bed in the other. The young adult male cousins found floor space in the game room and rolled out sleeping bags. The house was filled with music, laughter, food, and leisurely evenings with everybody gathered around the table for dinner — not just to eat (although that was a highlight), but to talk.

The conversation sparkled. Spirited political discussions were often a part of the table talk, but mostly the cousins enjoyed hearing the experiences of their grandparents. My parents, both eighty-five years old, told stories of their growing-up years and of their early marriage. They talked about the challenges and joys of raising six children. All of us laughed as Grandpa Afman recounted in detail the story of setting his eyes on Grandma for the first time at a roller rink. He proposed soon after they met, and the rest is history.

One memorable night, we gathered around the piano and sang Christmas carols — all the verses of many songs in the hymnbook that reminded us of long-ago days, growing up in our father's church.

J.P. had grown up calling my dad "Grandpa the Preacher." Perhaps it's because when your grandfather is a minister and you visit on weekends, you always go to church! It also helped to distinguish my father from Grandpa Bruce, Gene's stepfather, who took J.P. fishing and camping throughout his childhood.

As Gene and I carefully packed heirloom ornaments, along with cardboard Christmas decorations J.P. had created during his elementary school years, our nostalgia was offset by melancholy. All the relatives had gone home. The house was too quiet. We were alone. Once again I was faced with the harsh reality of my lost dreams for my son. As a few stray tears tumbled down my cheeks Gene said nothing, but he stopped packing up the decorations and held me for several silent minutes. We didn't need words to express our feelings. Unspoken heartache is a language all its own.

The ringing of the telephone interrupted the silence, and Gene picked up the receiver. Seconds later, he whispered urgently to me: "Get on an extension! Jason had to have emergency surgery!"

I breathlessly pulled a receiver to my ear and realized the call was from a corrections officer at the prison. "What happened?" I blurted into the mouthpiece.

"Ma'am, your son's appendix burst yesterday, and he had surgery at eleven o'clock last night. He's fine, and he'll probably be returned to the prison tomorrow."

Trying not to sound as upset as I was feeling, I answered, "Sir, my son had a ruptured appendix, with septic poisons exploding in his body, and he is being discharged from the hospital *tomorrow*?"

"Well, they don't keep them in the hospital very long these days. He'll be fine here at the prison," the officer said nonchalantly.

I was having trouble controlling my volcanic emotions. "Where is he?" I demanded.

"That's confidential information, ma'am. Your son is a maximum security inmate, and you are not allowed to know where he's located."

"You mean he has just had major surgery and we can't visit him?" I asked.

"That's right, ma'am. That would be a security risk. Don't go calling around trying to find out what hospital he's in."

I was choking back sobs as I gripped the receiver. Gene concluded the call and turned to console me. "Nothing about this experience gets any easier, does it?" he said, fresh tears of his own forming in his eyes. "At least we know he was taken to a civilian hospital and had surgery, and we know he's still alive." That thought provided a bit of consolation, but the next day we were told by the prison official that our son was still hospitalized. Each afternoon for the next four days we heard the same thing: "We think he'll be returned to the prison *tomorrow*."

Day after day, Gene and I prayed fervently that Jason would be given proper care in the wake of a serious medical emergency. I prayed for the doctors and nurses, and for the guards in his hospital room. Mostly I prayed for someone to see my son as a human being — a young man who was physically vulnerable and in need of expert care. I specifically prayed that God would send him someone who would look at him with eyes of compassion, who would care tenderly for both his physical and emotional needs.

After he was finally transported back to Hardee, where he spent five more days in the infirmary, Jason started a letter to us, detailing his ordeal.

> *The pain was so intense I was unable to lift myself off the upper bunk. I called for help, but the other inmates were in the TV room at the end of the hall and didn't hear me. Finally, one of the men realized I was in trouble and notified the prison guards that there was a medical emergency. They brought a wheelchair, and several men lifted me from my bed to the chair. I was burning up with fever and vomiting violently as I was wheeled to the infirmary.*
>
> *I tried to explain to the nurse practitioner on duty that I thought I had food poisoning. After quickly assessing my condition she said, "Son, you don't have food poisoning. You have appendicitis, and your appendix has probably burst already. You're going to the hospital!"*

*I was taken by ambulance to a twenty-five-bed facility fifteen minutes from the prison, and within a short time the medical team confirmed that my appendix had ruptured. They said they didn't have anyone on staff who could handle this type of emergency, so I was given pain medication and placed back in the ambulance for the ride to a larger hospital. At least five more hours passed before a surgical team finally performed an appendectomy and washed as much of the bacteria out of my abdominal cavity as they could before closing me up and putting me on antibiotics.*

*Since I'm a "lifer" and considered a high risk for flight, two corrections officers guarded my room at all times. And even though I was in constant pain after surgery and so weak I could hardly move, I had ankle shackles on with a chain between my legs twenty-four hours a day. Fortunately, the hospital staff treated me well — except for two people. I'm sure they struggled with their feelings about an inmate from a state penitentiary — one so "bad" he had to have armed guards around him 24/7.*

*One health care worker stood out from the rest. She told me her name was Nurse Betty, and whenever she was in my room, it was almost like having you with me, Mom. A day after my surgery, I had severe back pain and had been taken out of my bed and placed in a chair for a change in position. A couple of hours later, Nurse Betty came in to get me back to bed. She reached around me in a "hug" to help me stand, and although I let go after I was upright, she just kept holding me and told me to rest for a minute. For just that moment it was almost like having you giving me a big hug, Mom. I could feel tears in my eyes. I felt like God had sent an angel to my room at a time when I was hurting, needy, and lonely.*

*Over the next few days I experienced the difference between professionalism and compassion. Nurse Betty not only did an excellent job of caring for me, but she acted as if I was her own son. She didn't hesitate to help me in ways that no other hospital staff member even considered. She saw my needs, respected me as a human being who was suffering, and provided tangible aid.*

*In retrospect, I believe she treated everyone the way she treated me; compassion and mercy were in her heart long before I arrived at the hospital. But experiencing those qualities in such an up-close-and-personal way was like having God assure me that I wasn't forgotten by him — that I would be taken care of even though I was separated forever from daily life with my loved ones. In fact, Nurse Betty's agape love and merciful actions were unlike anything I had experienced outside of my own family in a very long time. She not only reminded me of you, Mom; she was like "Jesus with skin on" to me during those five days in the hospital. I can't adequately convey what this meant to me.*

When I read this part of the letter from my son, I realized that while I was praying for my boy, not feeling terribly confident that God was hearing my desperate pleas, he was demonstrating his mercy by providing Nurse Betty to be the mama I couldn't be to my critically ill child. God had not only provided Jason with a skilled nurse; he surprised me with someone who cared for my son as I would have cared for him myself. Nurse Betty was a woman who had sympathetic understanding of my son's distress and used all of her energy, training, and compassion to alleviate his pain and treat him like a human being who had worth and dignity. It was more than good fortune that placed Jason under the care of Nurse Betty. She was the answer to my prayers. I didn't know her name while I was praying for help for my son, but God did.

## Loving Our "Neighbor"

I used to think I understood the meaning of compassion. Certainly it meant feeling sorry for someone who was worse off than I was. Not so. As our family has experienced the kind of compassion that reflects

God's heart, I have come to believe that true mercy not only has "skin" on, but "feet" as well. Being merciful involves *action*.

Luke writes of a religious scholar who approached Jesus and asked, "What do I need to do to get eternal life?"[1] The scholar wasn't sincerely looking for salvation; rather, he was testing Jesus' knowledge of Old Testament law in order to try to discredit him as the Messiah promised by God. Jesus wisely turned the question back to the man and asked *him* what was written in the law and how he interpreted it. Quickly the man quoted a verse from the Old Testament: "That you love the Lord your God with all your passion and prayer and muscle and intelligence — and that you love your neighbor as well as you do yourself."[2] Jesus told him that he had just answered his original question: If he would love his neighbor this way, then he would truly "live."

The scholar wasn't satisfied. "Looking for a loophole, he asked, 'And just how would you define "neighbor"?' "[3] Jesus answered by relating the story of the Good Samaritan.[4]

Most of us are familiar with what happened to the Jewish man who was traveling between two towns when he was jumped by thieves. These violent men stripped him bare, beat him within an inch of his life, and left him in the road, severely injured. Jesus used the responses of three different people who came down that road after the crime to teach a clear lesson about the kind of love God asks us to show to others.

For a moment, put yourself in the battered man's shoes and imagine what must have been going on in his mind.

*I'm in agonizing pain! How could those cruel men do this to me? My face is in the dirt, and I can taste blood in my mouth. I feel like I could die of thirst, I'm so parched. Maybe I can pick myself up. No, my legs won't hold me. Oh God, please send someone to help me.*

Then out of the corner of his eye he sees the telltale robes of a religious man approaching.

*A man of faith! Oh, thank you, God. I know this person will take care of me.*

But the injured man watches in dismay as the one who represents his chance for rescue crosses to the other side of the road and passes by.

Then it happens again. Another religious man comes near, and the man who had been severely beaten tries to reach out, gasping for breath.

*I will surely die if someone doesn't help soon! Surely this man ...*

But he, too, looks the other way and doesn't lift a finger to help.

The story is about to shift in a surprising direction as a Samaritan comes down the road. Jews and Samaritans were cultural and religious enemies during the time when Jesus taught, and the scholar testing Jesus knew this. Any legal expert of that day would have argued that the person least likely to act mercifully toward the injured man would be the Samaritan.[5] Imagine, then, what the needy man must have thought.

*I see someone else coming now! But wait ... Oh no, he's a Samaritan. He certainly won't help me. I will surely die here on the side of the road. It looks like he's coming toward me. Please, God, may it not be just to kick me again. I can't take another blow. But no, this man is reaching toward me. I feel like I'm about to pass out, but I think he's lifting me. Yes, I see his donkey ...*

If I didn't know better, I'd say the man had "Nurse Betty" come to his rescue. The Samaritan had indeed saddled the Jew on the donkey, and then he transported him to a motel up the road.

*I must be delusional. I can hear the Samaritan talking to the innkeeper, asking him to take good care of me. He is promising to cover whatever it costs for me to get the care I need! He actually said, "Put this man's expenses on my tab." Can it be true that someone I would expect to hate me truly cares about me?*

After telling this story, Jesus turned to the scholar (who considered himself to be an expert on religion) and asked, "What do you think? Which of the three became a neighbor to the man attacked by robbers?"[6] The learned man couldn't get around that one. He responded: "The one who showed him mercy."[7]

The Hebrew word used for *mercy* in this passage connotes showing compassion (not pity) and extending help in the midst of a difficult circumstance. It involves showing immediate regard for the misery being experienced by someone in your path. It means *doing something* to help an individual in distress.

Jesus concluded his instruction by telling the scholar to go live his life the way the Samaritan (his "inferior") did. That had to be a bitter pill for a self-righteous man to swallow! Basically, Jesus was telling him to stop talking the talk and start walking the walk — and that's exactly what we all need to do.

I used to think I was a compassionate person who went out of my way to extend kindness to people in need. However, since Jason's incarceration I realize my "hand of mercy" came with conditions attached. I found it easy to help a single parent, a homeless person, or someone who was financially or physically needy. However, I wasn't so quick to notice someone struggling with an addiction, legal challenges, or sexual issues. Those things made me feel awkward, and I wondered what others would think of me for hanging out with "them."

Like the story of the Good Samaritan, the experience of Gail Knarr and her husband, Brian, reminds me that being self-righteous and consumed with outward appearances is not an option for someone who claims to love God. I must also "walk to the other side of the road" and show mercy in action to hurting fellow travelers, no matter who they are or what they've done.

## No Matter What — Gail's Story

I was always "the good girl." The oldest of four children, I felt it was my responsibility to set a good example for my siblings. I was raised in church and always followed "the rules" no matter where I was — home, school, church, with friends. I never smoked, drank, did drugs. I didn't even date in high school. I went to a Christian college and worked at a church camp in the summers. I remained sexually pure until my wedding night, and my husband was the love of my life, my best friend. Two years after we married, I gave birth to our beautiful daughter, Rachel, and was able to stay home to raise her, thus fulfilling my lifelong dream of being a wife and mother.

Life just got better and better. My husband became a music teacher at a middle school. We were active members of a church in our neighborhood where Brian was hired to be the music director; and we were able to serve together in church as I became part of the music ministry and served as the church drama director. We had lots of friends, and a number of people have told me that they looked to us as role models of marriage and parenting — the "perfect Christian family."

So what was I doing now, exactly twenty years after marrying the man of my dreams, sitting in the county health department waiting to be tested for HIV and other sexually transmitted diseases? Since I was practically the poster child for clean living and sexual purity, I was feeling more than a little arrogant. I looked around at the "derelicts" in the waiting room and began accusing them in my mind. "She's probably an addict." "He looks like he's high right now!" "I wonder if she even knows who the father of her child is."

God smacked me with a two-by-four. "Um, you're here too." I was immediately humbled, and when I looked around again, I could see each person as a child of God. "I hope she wasn't raped." "Maybe she doesn't have money for health insurance and has to come here for care." "Maybe I should pray for him to find a good job." In those moments my eyes were opened to how easy it is to judge people and how often I have rushed to judgment. In my "good girl" mind, it was way too easy to forget that we are all sinners, and no matter how perfect we try to be, sometimes we make mistakes, or bad things happen. Fortunately for me, God was showing me in a whole new way how he is always there, ready to pour out his mercy and love on us, no matter what.

Our family was in the midst of a "no matter what" situation that put us at the mercy of God and everyone we knew. Three months before that day in the health department waiting room, my world turned upside down. My husband was arrested in a county park for misdemeanor sexual assault on an undercover police officer. He had been caught in a police sting operation against public homosexual activity.

I had known of Brian's addiction to pornography and his struggle with same-sex attraction prior to our marriage. Many years later, I discovered evidence on our computer that he had been looking at porn again. He promised he would talk to a friend as an accountability partner and never go on those sites again. He was able to hold to the promise of never visiting the sites on our computer, but he never got around to the accountability. He had been hiding this shameful, secret part of his life for the past few years, trying to battle it completely alone. He said he had been terrified to open up to anyone else and expose himself to humiliation.

After his arrest on a Thursday afternoon, he tried to keep the information from Rachel and me, thinking he'd get through the last week of school, or at least the weekend, before saying anything. But he couldn't, and he told us that night at eleven thirty. He thought we would pack our bags and leave, but I never considered leaving. Brian has always been my best friend, and I reminded him I had vowed "for better or for worse." It was time to deal with the "worse." Rachel has been a Daddy's girl since the moment she was born, and she said to me, "I know I should hate him, but he's my daddy, I love him, and I want to stay here with him!" Our family was going to stick together, no matter what. (Fortunately, our tests were negative for STDs.)

Oddly, my first emotional reaction to Brian's news was relief. Up until now, I had been the only person in my husband's life who knew about his past. And even then, I didn't know his behavior had moved beyond just looking at porn to actual physical encounters. Nor did I know the initial factor that led him to this struggle: When he was ten or eleven years old, he had been introduced to pornography by a family friend and subsequently sexually molested by him over the course of the next several years. As a teenager, Brian had given his life to Christ and tried to lead the "perfect"

Christian life, but he continued to struggle with deep shame, low self-esteem, and a lot of confusion about himself. This led him down a path of secret trips to porn shops, movies, and public parks, as he sought to fill the lonely void that resulted from trying to bury his secrets even deeper. He says he actually knew deep down that in order to completely deal with the truth and be healed, he would probably have to be forced to hit rock bottom. He desperately hoped that wouldn't happen — but now, here he was: caught, arrested, handcuffed, humiliated.

Brian had been leading worship at our church for ten years by then, and he was well loved by the congregation. We wondered if all the goodwill from our friends would evaporate, like a well gone dry. What might happen next to make our nightmare even more horrific?

After Brian told Rachel and me about his arrest, he immediately called a dear friend, knowing she would be there for us, no matter what. She and Brian had worked closely together at the church, and for many years we had considered her and her family to be some of the people we wanted to "do life" with. Our friend came right over to our house, and we told her about Brian's arrest. The next day she went with Brian when he told our pastor, Steve Cordle. Pastor Steve showed himself to be a true friend and mentor, not just the good boss and colleague he had been for years. Even though Brian resigned from the church staff, Pastor Steve called or stopped by nearly every day for a couple of weeks.

The week after the arrest, Steve asked one of our friends to bring Brian a book to read — *Rebuilding Your Broken World*, by Gordon MacDonald. This author was a pastor who had had an affair and then had to work through the healing and restoration process. The dedication in the book read: "To Gail and 'the angels' — the inner core of many who have helped me rebuild my broken world." Pastor MacDonald's wife's name was Gail also. As we just stared at the book's dedication, our friend said, "I think this book is meant for you."

He was right! Within a week, we had our own "angels" —

four couples who came to know virtually everything about us. (Within a month we added three more people to that group.) They surrounded Brian and me with unconditional acceptance and showered us and our daughter with many forms of tangible support. Early on in the process, Pastor Steve told us he believed that the hard place we were experiencing would also be a test for the believers around us. How would the body of Christ handle such a difficult situation? Would we all survive, with God getting the glory?

Brian says that he had to be broken to the point where there was nothing but him and God, and that his healing will be only as complete as he is transparent with God and others. The decision to continue to remain totally open and accountable has not been made without some trepidation, as the church can be the most judgmental place; but our church congregation and the other Christian friends God has placed around us are passing the test with flying colors. We have many prayer warriors and supporters who have been with us through everything we've had to face — concerned and praying not only for Brian, but for Rachel and me as well. We have received nothing but love and support.

In addition to our inner circle of "angels," many others from both church and community demonstrated mercy to us in more ways than I can recount. After resigning from his jobs at both church and school, Brian was hired in sales at a furniture company and also picked up a night job at a hotel, where he did room service. Nevertheless, we faced significant financial challenges. Friends helped with Brian's legal fees and paid for his counseling. They even paid for our daughter's voice lessons and college application fees. One small group at church collected $150 cash to give us. One of the staff members dropped off two $60 supermarket gift cards "just in case" we might need them! Later in the year, right before Christmas, we received three checks from various people, each of whom told us God had put it on their heart to give us that gift. The checks totaled $2,000, an amount we sorely needed at the time. That same week, Rachel was called to the office at school to pick up an envelope addressed to her. Inside was an unsigned Christmas card containing a gift card to the mall worth $150. To this day we have no idea who was responsible for caring enough to make our daughter feel special during that difficult holiday season.

In addition to all the financial help, we were graced with moral support at all the right times. Brian had to go to many legal hearings, and often he didn't know until after he arrived at the courthouse that a proceeding had been canceled or moved to a different date. Nevertheless, at least one of our angels, usually several, showed up every time. If Brian had to be in court, they were there too. We also received an overwhelming number of cards and e-mails from people offering love and prayer. Brian actually put these notes in a scrapbook so he could look back at them when he was down.

For several weeks after his arrest, we were practically mobbed at church by people simply wanting to say they loved us and were praying for us. One couple came up to Brian after a service and said, "You have been such a blessing to us with your music and leadership here at church for so long. We are *blessed* to be able to pray for you now." Wow! These kinds of surprises, clearly divine interjections of grace, seemed to be never-ending during that very difficult time.

I wish I could say that all the pain is behind us, but I know we will experience more tight spots as we negotiate the road ahead. As part of his process of restoration, Brian continues to meet weekly with one of his accountability partners and periodically with one of our pastors at church. He was assigned a probation officer while completing a nine-month program that included performing fifty hours of community service. Pastor Steve connected Brian to a pastor-friend of his, Mark Ongley, who has a doctoral degree in counseling with a special focus on sexual brokenness. Pastor Mark has counseled a number of people who have been victims of sexual abuse and who have struggled with same-sex attraction. Brian met regularly with Mark for a year, and he admits that there are still temptations today. His sexual abuse caused him much confusion about his sexual identity, and he has learned through counseling that he was also craving acceptance by males. He thought he could get this through same-sex encounters, but he continues to learn that this is a lie — that he is accepted by God and men just as he is, without having to "measure up" for his perceived lack of worth.

While his male "angel" friends were shocked at first by Brian's past behavior, it did not change their opinion of him. In fact, it caused them to pray for him all the more and to freely give him the love he craved. They have been with him every step of the way — crying, laughing, listening, and just accompanying him through everything he's faced. When temptations come up today, he says he practices reminding himself that he doesn't need to act out in the destructive ways of the past. As he risks sharing his struggles with the guys who truly love him, he learns that he is unconditionally accepted by God and complete in him.

A few weeks after Brian was arrested, we were at the church camp we attend as a family each summer, hoping against hope that we could enjoy a respite from the intense turmoil we were going through. Instead, we got word that a TV news report at home had mentioned Brian's name, fueling rumors that just made everything feel more out of control for us. It felt like the whole world was crashing down around us. Later that night, we witnessed one of the most spectacular sunsets we had ever seen on Lake Erie during our twenty years of marriage. It was as though God was saying, "I know you think your life is in shambles, but I have everything under control. Look at what I painted for you tonight!"

I continue to keep my eyes open for these gifts of grace and to thank God when I notice them. I have no reason to doubt that he is watching over us with loving care because of countless reminders like that sunset and because of all the mercy and generosity shown to our family while we have lived between a rock and a hard place. Our church family and friends are a living example of the body of Christ — the church "being" the church. Because of the ways they have continually displayed God's grace to us, we know that God's goodness and mercy are deeper and wider than we ever imagined.[8]

## Mercy Matters

When we love others the way Jesus taught us to, something good happens, not only to the people we love, but also to us. Authentic compassion and genuine mercy never say, "You poor thing! I feel sorry for you." God's love transforms us into people who have a better way of meeting the needs of others. Our vision sharpens and our hearts soften, making us the kind of people who actively respond to suffering instead of looking away or walking to the other side of the street. We start to view "interruptions" or detours on the road as divine appointments — unexpected opportunities to practice our theology in tangible ways.

In the early weeks following Jason's arrest, Gene and I had no idea how we would be able to afford sizable monthly payments to his attorney. We had already made a large down payment on his legal services, exhausting our savings and tapping into our retirement funds. We had agreed to pay the rest of the fee in monthly installments over the next year.

One afternoon as I sifted through the stack of mail that had just been delivered, the return address on one of the envelopes caught my eye. It was from Jan. She had been my best friend in high school, and we have maintained our friendship ever since. "Carol, I know these are challenging financial times for you and Gene," she wrote, "and I'm enclosing a check for you to have on hand for when you need it." I looked at the large amount of money and gulped. I called her to explain that I didn't want to accept a gift of that magnitude. It didn't seem right. But she insisted. "Just put the money in the bank, and you'll know it's there in case you need it."

Month by month we had no idea if we would earn a sufficient amount to pay the attorney — but each time the installment was due, one of our God-surprises was that we had enough money to pay the bill. Sometimes we squeaked by as we balanced our budget, but there was always *just enough*.

Even though we were eventually able to return the money Jan gave us, the knowledge that we had an emergency fund eased our minds beyond description. She saw our need, and instead of looking the other way while saying, "I'm praying for you," Jan walked to our side of the road. She extended her hand with the gift of security in the form of a check to be used when and if it was needed.

Compassion and mercy come to me more easily now that I'm a mama with shattered dreams over a son who will be incarcerated for the rest of his life. And I no longer apologize for my tears or try to hide any of my emotions. I'm comforted by these words from the Bible: "If your heart is broken, you'll find GOD right there; if you're kicked in the gut, he'll help you catch your breath."[9] I've discovered that one of the most important ways God is "right there" in times of need is through the kindness and mercy of other people. He uses folks like Nurse Betty; my best friend, Jan; and even strangers and supposed "enemies" to help us make it through the most difficult challenges of our lives. And he tells us to do the same for the hurting people we find on the roads we travel.

## EXPLORING YOUR OWN GRACE PLACE

It often feels easier to give mercy than to receive it. But when we're in the middle of a situation we can't fix on our own, the tangible compassion of a fellow traveler can be a humbling and delightful surprise on our journey. Sometimes this gift of mercy comes through kind eyes instead of harsh judgment. It can come in the form of emotional or financial support, a handwritten note, or a bouquet of flowers. It can be as simple as a bag of groceries or as major as a large check. Someone sees our need, goes out of his or her way to understand our situation, and does something concrete to make sure our condition is improved. The action of a mercy giver is often a complete surprise to the recipient. My son calls it "being like Jesus with skin on," because the result brings relief, hope, and healing. We begin to see light at the end of the tunnel, and the person who flips this switch on is our "angel in disguise."

1. How do you define a "tight spot" in life? Have you found yourself in one that was temporarily challenging, or has it permanently altered the rest of your life?

2. When you are in a difficult situation, do you like to be left alone, or do you appreciate receiving assistance from a caring person? Why?

3. *Mercy* has many definitions. Which of the following descriptions means the most to you? (1) to ease distress or pain; (2) to show compassion to another; (3) to forgive a wrong; (4) to receive a kindness from someone who has more power or resources than you do. Describe a time in your life when you experienced one of these forms of mercy.

4. Sometimes we feel more comfortable showing mercy to people who are financially challenged or to those who are facing health problems or whose difficulties are due to circumstances entirely beyond their control. But when someone is struggling with an addiction or has committed a crime, or when their situation is

in some other way "socially unacceptable," we often don't know how to respond. What did you learn from Gail and Brian Knarr's story? What aspect of the way people demonstrated mercy to them impacted you the most? What can our churches learn from the Knarrs' difficult experience?

5. In the story of the Good Samaritan, the man who received help from an unlikely source was "surprised by mercy." He was in great need, and he received extraordinary care. From your own experience, do you believe the person receiving mercy is the one most blessed, or is the giver of mercy the one who reaps the greatest reward? Why do you think so?

6. This chapter began with a quote from Corrie ten Boom: "What did you do today that only a Christian would have done?" Jesus said, "I was hungry and you fed me, I was thirsty and you gave me a drink, I was homeless and you gave me a room, I was shivering and you gave me clothes, I was sick and you stopped to visit, I was in prison and you came to me."[10] Take a few minutes to list the people within your sphere of influence who are having a difficult time right now. Next to each name write down one thing you could do to show mercy to that individual or family. Remember, mercy doesn't need to cost a lot. Mercy sees a need, evaluates the resources available, and chooses to get involved in a personal, tangible way. How can you be "Jesus with skin on" to someone in your path?

# CHAPTER 3

# LONGING FOR A BETTER LIFE

## SURPRISED BY CONTENTMENT

> The happiness which brings enduring worth to life is not
> the superficial happiness that is dependent on circumstances.
> It is the happiness and contentment that fills the soul even
> in the midst of the most distressing circumstances and
> the most bitter environment. It is the kind of happiness that
> grins when things go wrong and smiles through the tears.
> **Dr. Billy Graham**

It was Labor Day weekend. I was speaking at a church in London, Ontario, and we had flown from Tampa into Detroit and rented a car in order to lower our travel expenses. The most direct route was to take I-94 East and cross over the St. Clair River on the Blue Water Bridge from Port Huron, Michigan, and go through customs in Sarnia, Ontario before driving another hour to London.

It took longer to get through customs than when we lived in Port Huron three years earlier. The security measures slowed traffic to a halt as we presented our passports and responded to the mandatory questions at the border between the U.S. and Canada.

✦ What is your citizenship?

65

      &#10070; What is your purpose for entering the country?

      &#10070; How long will you be staying?

      &#10070; Are you carrying any firearms?

I had been looking forward to this trip. Gene and I had often crossed this border during our twenty-six years of living in the area. Our son was raised in Port Huron, and we had many friends in both countries.

The weekend was filled with catching up with old friends between the four church services that took place on Saturday night and Sunday morning. It was a joy to speak at the church in London and to celebrate the beginning of their fall season of ministry.

We knew our return trip would be more leisurely, so we planned ahead to visit Gene's best friend, Dan, and his wife, Joan, on the way back through Port Huron. Their married son, a young attorney, was visiting that weekend, so we were anticipating the added delight of seeing Carl and Julie and their now six-year-old twin boys. But something came up that we didn't anticipate. Gene later journaled about this visit.

He was not my son, but he could have been. Blue eyes. Straight teeth. Flashing smile. Quick to discuss everything — politics, Christianity, history, college, raising kids. His winsome personality and positive attitude about life were disarming and contagious. He was helpful with his children and looked lovingly at his wife. His fingers were often entwined in hers in an affectionate, lingering manner.

Carl was trim, athletic, confident, clean-shaven, and stylish. He was articulate and energetic as he talked of participating in a fifteen-mile run that morning and about his involvement in the men's ministry at his church. He had been asked to serve on the board of elders and was juggling that responsibility with his job as a lawyer for a new bank in Pennsylvania. I was captivated by his maturity, discernment, and wisdom.

I found my mind wandering while observing the casual interaction of the group gathered around a table full of finger foods. Carol was placing cheese, crackers, and fruit on her plate while engaging in a vigorous conservation with Joan. I felt fortunate to have made such a first-rate choice in a wife when I was only twenty-two-years old. She seemed to get more beautiful with age, and I realized that time and trouble had bonded us in ways that defied description.

Later I watched Carl play catch with his boys in the front yard. As he moved to return to the house, one of the twins, pretending to be the "voice" of his gerbil-like stuffed animal, pulled his father back into the game. It was a playful, spontaneous moment — a father and his son having fun together.

Without warning, an unexpected emotion leaped into my heart like a stranger invading my personal space. I instantly recognized it as jealousy. I hadn't seen Carl in several years — not since he was a teenager in the church youth group — and I realized he had grown into a young man not unlike my own son. Except for one important difference. My son is in prison for the rest of his life.

Wasn't Jason the energized and articulate young man I saw before me now? Wasn't he going to use his education, leadership, and potential in a great career the way Carl was doing? Wasn't he going to be a great dad who interacted with his children in meaningful ways? Wasn't he going to make a good living and take care of the needs of his family? Wasn't my son going to take his kids to the movies on Friday nights, have "date night" with his wife on Saturday nights, and take his family to church on Sundays?

Carl is the picture of what I envisioned my boy would look like at the same age. In reality, I see my son behind barbed wire in a blue uniform with white stripes on the sides of his trousers, wearing black shoes and sporting a regulation haircut. Instead of meeting his family for days at the beach, followed by engaging conversations in our home, I see him in an institution where there are big grey concrete block buildings arranged on a grid with guarded sidewalks between them. We don't have iced lemonade and fancy finger foods during our visits. We get our meals out of vending machines and from the prison canteen.

Momentarily, the green-eyed monster took a bite out of a much-anticipated visit. It took some effort to shove that emotion aside so

*I could enjoy every moment of our remaining time with these valued and caring friends.*

## Pity Parties and Meltdowns

While I am not always sure what contentment looks or feels like in the "new normal" that has become our life, I do know that the opposite of contentment is dissatisfaction. When we give in to that state of mind, it allows jealousy and self-pity to take root. Without warning we find ourselves resentful — and sometimes coveting the favorable life, excellent job, successful family, financial rewards, or apparent happiness of someone else.

I'm the most apt to throw a pity party when I dwell on our losses since Jason's incarceration. While other families are getting together for shared meals on weekends or taking trips to amusement parks with their children and grandchildren, I'm standing in line at the prison — again — waiting to visit my son in a restricted, impersonal room filled with other inmates and their loved ones. As much as I look forward to spending time with my boy, I occasionally give in to envy when I see other families doing normal activities.

Sometimes my anguish comes out "sideways" — and it's not uncommon for the person closest to me to get hit with the shrapnel of my meltdowns. Fortunately, I don't have them often anymore, but when I do, they are usually triggered by something innocuous, like an offhand comment from a normally good-natured husband.

After Jason's arrest something slowly changed in our marriage. Gene and I were short with each other. The "small stuff" became "big stuff," and little disagreements sometimes escalated into full-blown, loud arguments. At first, neither one of us could understand what was happening.

One day, Gene entered our big walk-in closet and said, in an uncharacteristically surly tone, "I just don't understand why you can't get rid of clothes you haven't worn in a year. This closet is a mess, and I don't like living like this!"

I was livid. "How can you say that? The rest of our home is spotlessly clean, and all I ask for is one closet where I can toss my personal belongings without your criticism. I'm sick of this house *and* this closet. In fact, I'm sick of *you*! I'm mad at you! I'm tired of your mean comments! If you don't like the looks of this closet, then don't walk through the door! You are not welcome in this space!"

By this time I was yelling through tears, and they kept coming and coming, until I was sobbing. Gene stood there with a startled look on his face. I took a step closer to him and pounded on his chest as I screamed, "I hate this closet as much as you do! I hate these clothes and shoes! *I hate my life!*" Spotting an old silk-flower arrangement that had been placed on a shelf in the closet, I blurted out, "And I hate that stupid plant too!"

Gene put his arms around me and waited patiently for my wailing to subside. I had quit beating on his chest and had relaxed into his embrace. "What just happened between us isn't really about the closet, is it?" he asked softly.

"No," I murmured. Gene knew that my explosion was about our son. "I miss him so much," I admitted. "I'm devastated by what's happened. I'm angry at God for letting J.P. kill a man. I'm sad for the family of that man and for all of their losses and our losses. I'm miserable, and I've been taking it out on you. I'm trying to have faith in God and to keep believing he is in control of this mess, but I'm beginning to question that. And I hate myself for having these doubts about him."

"Me too," Gene said, with tears in his baby-blue eyes.

"I'm sorry for reacting like this. Will you forgive me?" I said, while holding on to him tightly.

"Yes," Gene responded. "Will you forgive me too?"

I nodded. And over time, we learned that it's better to talk to each other frankly about the real issues we are facing than to get mad over petty irritations that become full-blown fights — all because we are dealing with a challenge that threatens to suck the life out of us. Once we "got" that the Enemy would love to destroy our marriage as a result of our son's situation, he became the *real* enemy. We now know that when little issues spark small disagreements that could put us at serious odds with each other, it's time to pause long enough to recognize what's happening and remind one another: "This isn't the real problem, is it?" Rather than pulling us apart, our greatest challenges have pressed us into a safe place with each other where we can be honest about what we are feeling — including our grief, anger, fear, and self-pity — without judging the other person.

## A Life Well Spent

One night, Gene and I were watching TV when a well-known television personality interrupted his normal programming to announce that the beloved evangelist, Billy Graham, was about to celebrate his ninetieth birthday. He urged viewers to e-mail birthday greetings to Dr. Graham and to include a note about a significant way their lives had been impacted by this well-known preacher. I was intrigued by the passion and tenderness expressed by the secular media host.

After the program ended, I went to my computer and did an Internet search on Billy Graham's name. It didn't take long to recognize one of the secrets of this man's profound and productive life: Dr. Graham has practiced contentment as a lifestyle. In his own words: "The happiness for which our souls ache is one undisturbed by success or failure, one which will root deeply inside us and give inward relaxation, peace, and contentment, no matter what the surface problems may be. That kind of happiness stands in need of no outward stimulus."[1]

A few months ago, Gene and I flew into Charlotte, North Carolina, for an evening event at an area church. Our host picked us up at the airport and announced that we had plenty of time to stop by the Billy Graham Evangelistic Headquarters, where we could visit the Billy Graham Library as well as Ruth Graham's grave. We eagerly agreed to this unexpected opportunity. Just a year earlier, the Billy Graham Evangelistic Association had sent a producer and a videographer to our home to interview us for a cameo testimony insert on their prime-time TV

Christmas special. They also filmed us with Jason at the prison, and our hearts are tender toward their ministry.

Once on the grounds, we toured the common areas, viewed the photo gallery of the life and times of the Graham family, and were reminded of the profound impact of this global ministry. We also walked through the home where Billy Graham grew up. Then we silently made our way down the path to the Prayer Garden, where Ruth Bell Graham is buried. I learned that her plywood coffin was handmade by inmates in Louisiana at Angola, the largest maximum security prison in the U.S., where revival has transformed the entire prison compound in recent years as men have given their lives to Christ. At Angola, also called "The Farm," 90 percent of the inmates have sentences that will end only with their own deaths.

When Warden Burl Cain came to this state penitentiary in 1995, he discovered that many of the inmates who died were unclaimed by their family members, so they were buried in cardboard boxes and placed in graves dug by a backhoe, with no funeral services. The new warden instituted a program that allowed inmates to make simple wooden coffins and be buried at Point Lookout Cemetery on the prison grounds. He said, "We decided to build a horse-drawn carriage and pull the coffins to the cemetery ... and the inmates could preach [the funeral messages]."[2] Hundreds of the more than five thousand inmates line the road leading to the cemetery and show their respect when the remains of a fellow inmate are being transported on this carriage to his final resting place. This new practice has brought dignity to the deaths of the prisoners who have no next of kin to pick up their remains — which is about half of all inmates who die at Angola.

When Franklin Graham, Billy and Ruth's son, visited this prison in 2005, he saw one of the simple coffins the inmates had made — a birch plywood box lined with a foam mattress pad covered with fabric. The cost of each coffin: $215. Knowing how deeply his parents valued simplicity and eschewed extravagance or fanfare, he asked the inmates if they would build two more of the birch burial boxes — one for each of his parents. The inmates agreed.

When Ruth Bell Graham passed away, her lifelong value system was reflected in her final resting place: a plain, no-frills box, crafted by prisoners much like my son — "lifers" who find contentment in knowing that this world is not their final home. As I stood at Mrs. Graham's gravesite, I was moved to tears — touched by the reminder that, though our time on earth is fleeting, a life well spent can be lived on either side of the razor wire. A genuine peace and contentment filled my heart.

## A Man Named Paul

I have always been intrigued with the apostle Paul. When our son was born, we named him Jason Paul. His middle name was chosen for two reasons. My mother's name is Pauline, and my love for her is deep, so I wanted to honor my godly mother by including a portion of her name in the name of her firstborn grandson. But the second reason for choosing Paul as a middle name was because the Bible character by the same name was such an inspiration to me. The apostle Paul was a man of fierce determination, great influence, and passion, who did not let his past dictate what his future would become. Gene and I knew that his name had great strength and meaning.

The life story of Paul reads like an epic novel. His résumé was something to be proud of in his culture; his heritage included being "a Hebrew of Hebrews." No doubt his peers were impressed with Paul's family tree because his descendents could trace their ancestry all the way back to the ancient Israelite tribe of Benjamin. He was distinguished by his legalism — a strict Pharisee, acclaimed for his zeal in persecuting Christians. Paul even spoke of his "faultless" life, which referred to his former self-righteousness when he was known as Saul, the name given to him at birth.[3]

But his life dramatically changed on the road to Damascus. He was no doubt carrying a list of suspected Christians he was out to get when a brilliant light blinded him and a voice from heaven spoke.

> He fell to the ground and heard a voice saying to him, "Saul! Saul! Why are you persecuting me?"

"Who are you, lord?" Saul asked.

And the voice replied, "I am Jesus, the one you are persecuting!"[4]

Stop. Rewind. Who was Saul persecuting? Christians. Yet the voice from heaven asked, "Why are you persecuting *me*?" That question brings peace to my spirit. In other words, when anybody comes after me with a hurtful, harassing, or demeaning attack, it's as if God is saying, "She belongs to *me!* If you have targeted her, you are hounding *me!* I have a covenant relationship with the person you are pursuing, so if you are bullying her, you'll have to deal with *me!*" And suddenly I can breathe. Relax. Experience peace. If I press into my Rock when I'm afraid, I find contentment.

After Saul's conversion, he was renamed Paul — and the rest of his transformed and purposeful life included controversy, multiple missionary journeys, close friendships and ministry relationships, incarceration, and lots of writing. Paul is credited with writing thirteen books in the New Testament, and many of those manuscripts were completed when he was chained to a soldier of the Roman Guard. No wonder we read at the end of Paul's letter to the Philippians: "All the Christians here, especially the believers who work in the palace of Caesar, want to be remembered to you."[5] During Paul's incarceration many people around him must have come to faith. His times of imprisonment were not wasted.

One of the great stories from his life is recorded in Acts 16. He and Silas were arrested because their mission work was negatively impacting the income of citizens who were exploiting a demon-possessed girl for profit. Before an earthquake freed the two men in the middle of the night, they were praying and singing hymns to God while other prisoners listened.[6] Paul's peace under pressure and the resulting positive impact on the people around him remind me that God is eager to surprise me with unexpected outcomes. In addition to the demon-possessed girl being freed from her bondage, a businesswoman named Lydia came to faith and a jailer was converted, which resulted in a Christian church starting in Philippi.

I was surprised to learn that Paul had more to say about contentment than any other contributor to the Bible. After all, in addition to being harassed and imprisoned for his new faith, he had a "thorn in the flesh," which could have led him to be bitter and full of self-pity. Instead, it became a paradoxical blessing. Paul's vulnerability is never described in detail, but it humbled him enough to remind him to be constantly dependent on God.

> I was given the gift of a handicap to keep me in constant touch with my limitations. Satan's angel did his best to get me down; what he in fact did was push me to my knees. No danger then of walking around high and mighty! At first I didn't think of it as a gift, and begged God to remove it. Three times I did that, and then he told me,
>
> > My grace is enough; it's all you need.
> > My strength comes into its own in your weakness.
>
> Once I heard that, I was glad to let it happen. I quit focusing on the handicap and began appreciating the gift. It was a case of Christ's strength moving in on my weakness Now I take limitations in stride, and with good cheer, these limitations that cut me down to size — abuse, accidents, opposition, bad breaks. I just let Christ take over! And so the weaker I get, the stronger I become.[7]

## Hard-Won Peace

The dictionary defines *contentment* as "the quality or state of being contented," and *contented* is defined as "feeling or showing satisfaction with one's possessions, status, or situation."[8] One of the key ingredients of contentment is accepting the hand dealt to us in life, our place in this world, the people in our circle, and the resources we have. Frankly, if my level of contentment could be monitored on a meter that measures satisfaction and acceptance, I know there are days when neither attitude would even register. Instead, my dissatisfaction would be off the charts.

Paul's example of dealing with adversity over more than three decades of his life as a Christ-follower encourages me, because throughout his writings Paul describes the inner peace that we can *learn* to cultivate, regardless of circumstances. Even while imprisoned — again — by the Romans, he wrote,

> Actually, I don't have a sense of needing anything personally. I've learned by now to be quite content whatever my circumstances. I'm just as happy with little as with much, with much as with little. I've found the recipe for being happy whether full or hungry, hands full or hands empty. Whatever I have, wherever I am, I can make it through anything in the One who makes me who I am.[9]

From a place of complete confidence in the God who transcends all human experiences, Paul urged the early Christians to be "content with what you have; for He Himself has said, 'I will never desert you, nor will I ever forsake you.'"[10]

As parents of a lifer, Gene and I find ourselves wondering (and sometimes worrying!) about how prisoners, including our son, will be cared for as our country continues to experience a deep financial crisis that has negatively affected the lives of almost everybody in our society. As there is less and less money for the upkeep of prisons, the salaries of prison employees, the health care and meal quality of inmates, and the education of the incarcerated, how will the United States take care of the nearly two and a half million inmates in our country?

Another thought that steals my contentment as a mom is wondering what will happen to our son after Gene and I get old and die. That may seem like a morbid thought, but the reality is in your face when you have a child with a life sentence. Younger family members will one day be responsible for making sure there is enough money in Jason's account to cover his basic needs. J.P. once wrote to us about some of the added indignities inmates experience when they don't have anyone looking out for them on the outside.

*When prisoners have no family member who deposits money in their inmate account, they wear footwear provided by the Department of Corrections — little slip-on shoes called "bo-bos" (pronounced with long o's) that are three sizes too small or three sizes too big. When a man's shoes are too big, he looks like a little child wearing his father's shoes — just shuffling along so they don't fall off. When the footwear is too small, the inmates' feet are cramped into little slippers that only cover their toes, with their heels hanging out over the backs of the shoes. Often, when a hole is worn through the sole of a bo-bo, a large piece of cloth tape is applied instead of having the shoe replaced.*

*The trousers we wear are often patched or extended with six or more inches of material to make them longer. Towels are sewn together from two, or sometimes three, pieces of old towels.*

*These little things take away part of our dignity — and if we let these common practices get to us, it produces discontent.*

Any contentment I experience can go right out the window when I start dwelling on my concerns about who will provide for and care deeply about my son for the rest of his life. I don't have a chance for peace of mind unless I truly believe that my God — my son's God — will never desert him. I must continually practice following more of Paul's excellent advice:

Don't fret or worry. Instead of worrying, pray. Let petitions and praises shape your worries into prayers, letting God know your concerns. Before you know it, a sense of God's wholeness, everything coming together for good, will come and settle you down. It's wonderful what happens when Christ displaces worry at the center of your life.[11]

The challenges my son is experiencing as a guilty man imprisoned for committing murder don't compare to the extreme challenges Paul faced as a Christian unjustly persecuted in Roman society. But Jason, like Paul, is learning that contentment is not just a feeling, and it's not dependent on his circumstances. Ironically, my incarcerated son is teaching me the true meaning of contentment.

In one of his letters, Jason described the stark reality of his day-to-day life, the unexpected benefits of simplicity, and his hard-won peace.

*All of my possessions MUST fit into a small one-foot-high and one-and-a-half-feet-deep and two-and-a-half-feet-long steel lockbox. All of the earthly possessions I care about are placed in this box. If what I'm saving doesn't make it inside the box, it gets confiscated by the prison security staff. My inmate friends and I have become masters at packing our goods tightly.*

*I'm also learning to live comfortably with very little. I've seen men kill and be killed for what's in these small boxes, whether it's their photo album of loved ones, their canteen items (soda pop, candy bars, chips, or a Honey Bun), their smokes, their legal paperwork, or their books. I'm discovering it's good not to have too many things I can't afford to lose, because on any given day I could lose everything. In some ways it's easier to live with having so little to protect or worry about. It's like camping, but there's no tent to put up and no campfire to build. Of course, there are also no marshmallows to melt or s'mores to eat, no hikes in the woods, and no family to join me in sing-alongs around the fire.*

*Mom, this is not the life I would have chosen. With all my heart, I long for the "burden" of a career, the challenge of house and car payments, the warmth of a home, and, most of all, the joy of being with my family — loving them, providing for them, and nurturing them. But I know now that I don't need a lot of "things" to make me happy. I'm beginning to understand what the apostle Paul meant when he wrote that "true godliness with contentment is itself great wealth. After all, we brought nothing with us when we came into the world, and we can't take anything with us when we leave it."[12] The simplicity of having almost nothing and of watching fellow inmates take care of each other's everyday needs brings a different kind of serenity to the spirit.*

*I'm learning to take life one day at a time, sometimes one hour, minute, or second at a time. When depressing thoughts envelop me, it's important for me to break the day down into smaller fragments.*

*I'm also learning to enjoy the pleasures of this moment—a conversation, a letter, a phone call, a visit, a prayer, a hug—for the pleasures they are. Tomorrow has plenty of problems of its own— things I can't do anything about. I'm learning to choose prayer over worry. I try to live in the moment and enjoy what this day has to offer and to have a thankful heart. If you are observant, there are many things to be grateful for in every event, and even in every challenge.*

*Experiencing contentment in my current circumstances is a daily choice, and some days are much harder than others. But I find that my times of pain lead me to my most intimate times of prayer and communion with God. By practicing gratefulness for the way I am blessed and provided for, I am learning to be content.*

I know there are days when Jason is tempted to give in to anger, bitterness, and jealousy. I have those temptations too. But I'm encouraged as I see him trying to internalize this truth from the New Testament: "Give your entire attention to what God is doing right now, and don't get worked up about what may or may not happen tomorrow. God will help you deal with whatever hard things come up when the time comes."[13] When I choose to live one day at a time instead of trying to make it through my son's entire life sentence, I'm surprised by contentment. The secret of this contentment is to focus on joining God where he is at work today — and that does take practice.

When I was a young teacher, I met Cathy Gallagher, and it didn't take long for our friendship to develop. At that time, neither of us knew we would both face difficult circumstances that would challenge our faith and disrupt our comfortable lives. Cathy and I have shared celebrations and sorrows together, and I know you'll be inspired by her story.

## A Treasure Hunt — Cathy's Story

I had just received my last paycheck and was officially unemployed — again. This time I was a casualty of a corporate buyout. The sickening feeling in my gut was all too familiar. From experience I knew that relinquishing this job meant watching another career dream shatter and another piece of my identity fall away. I was heartsick over having to start over — again.

I thought about the circumstances that had brought me to a management position in this company. More than a decade earlier, I had been reveling in self-employment as a trainer and consultant. I loved my business, and I was good at it. I had started it in a way that you read about in success books. After winning the "salesperson of the year" award from my previous employer, I sensed it was time to venture out on my own, and I turned my employer into my first client. Relinquishing that job was fun because I chose to do it, and I did it in a way that was a win-win for my employer and me.

Eight years later, I moved from Wisconsin to California to accept a marketing job for a start-up company filled with enthusiastic risk takers with big dreams and high hopes, just like mine. Within six months, however, my position was eliminated. I spent countless hours figuring out how to file an unemployment claim, trying to understand the rules in the thick "Claimants' Handbook," and maintaining the mountain-sized stack of paperwork related to my job search. I felt perpetually overwhelmed by the complex unemployment insurance system and dismayed by the meager results of the seemingly endless labor required to seek labor!

Eventually my job-hunting efforts paid off. I headed back across the country to work for a Missouri-based company — the one I was now about to leave because of the buyout. I was dejected at the thought of joining the ranks of the unemployed — again. But as I cleaned out my desk, I reminded myself to trust God's plan and to walk by faith and not by sight. While I was not content with my circumstances, I did feel a surprising sense of inner peace.

Right then, my phone rang. When I answered it, I heard words that made me smile. I had landed the job I had recently interviewed for with a company nearby. I was confident that God's plan was unfolding. Within two weeks, however, I received a second offer from an employer that I felt was a better fit. I moved to Michigan to accept the new position. But nothing went as I expected, and six months later I was unemployed — again.

I spent four months jobless before landing another management position — which lasted all of six weeks. Back to the unemployment line I went, feeling devastated.

Six more months passed, and my unemployment benefits in Michigan had just run out. When an unexpected offer suddenly came my way, I wasn't sure what I thought of God's sense of humor. God has made everyone an expert at something, and he made me an expert at unemployment. I guess he thought I was spending so much time standing in line and filling out paperwork at the state unemployment office that I might as well get paid for it!

As I reluctantly walked through the door he opened for me there, my feelings were a jumbled-up mess. I plastered a smile on my face and tried to look thankful that I had a full-time job with good benefits, but I silently questioned God. "Why *this* door, Lord? Why this job with a salary of less than half of what I was making? Why an entry-level position with traditional hours, doing work unlike anything I've done before that doesn't even seem suited to the gifts and skills you have given me?"

I had longed for what I considered to be a prestigious and glamorous opportunity, the type of work I had done in sales or marketing or training that involved travel, challenges, excitement, and high wages. I was finding it difficult to be truly thankful and content, and I felt guilty for having such an ungrateful heart. In short, I was making myself miserable, and I certainly was not much fun to be around.

It didn't take me long to realize that I had to make a choice. I could either continue being discontent or I could begin to uncover the hidden gems in my new, unfamiliar work environment. I made a decision to go on a treasure hunt, intentionally looking for treasures — and in the process I learned more about contentment than I could have ever imagined.

I used to think that contentment was just a guise for giving up on high hopes, desires, and dreams. I actually considered it a weakness. Now I realize that contentment is just the opposite. It is the strong foundation that keeps hope, dreams, and desires alive and vibrant and that helps us identify new paths to take when we are in unfamiliar or unwanted circumstances. I heard a statement in a sermon long ago that I now understand from firsthand experience: *If you aren't content with where you are now or with what you have now, how will you be content somewhere else or with anything else?*

The second gem I unearthed during those early days in a job that didn't fit my dream has proved to be invaluable. Contentment, I learned, is a hallmark of living fully in the present, not in the past or future. When I stopped longing for the type of job and career I'd had in the past, I began to see opportunities in the here and now. For example, I have a master's degree in teaching, and I love teaching adults. Because my position at the unemployment agency is a day job, I was able to pursue and accept an opportunity to teach evenings at a university, which I've now been doing for five years. I also enrolled in a Bible college and slowly began working toward a Bachelor of Christian Ministry degree I'd long desired, and seven years later I graduated. I turned my pain and experience into a six-week Bible study for the unemployed that puts hope back into the hearts of people just like me. Had God opened a different door for me, I would not have been able to do these things.

Perhaps the most important principle I have discovered is that discontent breeds more discontent, but contentment generates joy and satisfaction. I have been working at Michigan's unemployment office for eight years now. I have been promoted and enjoy helping newer workers resolve problems with unemployment claims. I am content with where I am because it is where God put me. With the crisis in the auto industry, Michigan's unemployment rate has been higher than any other state's for several years. At a time when thousands of others my age or younger have been standing in unemployment lines and scrambling to find work for months, even years, I am working mandatory overtime. At the age of sixty-two, I am in a good job that God handpicked for me, and I am using the skills and gifts he gave me in ways I never anticipated.

Looking back, I see that, like the apostle Paul, I had to *learn* how to be content. I'm still learning. This leg of my spiritual journey began with my willingness to make the choice to go on a treasure hunt for gems of contentment. The riches I have unearthed on this journey have shaped my present, and I'm confident they will continue to impact my future in surprising ways.[14]

## The Joy of Simplicity

When God asks us to do something outside our usual definition of "normal" and invites us to view our circumstances through his eyes, it's hard to move forward unless we have confidence in his care. When we trust that he is in sovereign control of our hard place, we can press into a grace place where there is rest, peace, and a different kind of contentment — a satisfaction not based on financial security or physical comfort, a serenity that can only be experienced when our focus is on a life beyond this one. It's a life free from prison bars, concrete walls, physical pressures, debilitating jealousy, emotional challenges, mental anxiety, and disappointing or hurtful people.

Gene and I have decided that when we die, we don't want money to be spent on lavish funerals and elaborate "burial boxes." We plan to contact the Louisiana State Penitentiary and order our own birch ply-wood coffins from the Angola prisoners. After all, because we believe something more is coming beyond this life, we prefer to have our left-over financial resources spent to further God's kingdom agenda rather than on making us look good in expensive, fancy boxes that people who happen to attend our funerals will see only once.

It's a freeing thing to experience the joy of simplicity. Our son is teaching us this principle by the way he lives his life. We're discovering that contentment comes as a divine surprise when we embrace our current situation with grateful hearts.

## EXPLORING YOUR OWN GRACE PLACE

Sometimes it's easiest to understand what contentment is when we're not thinking about it. When "all is well" in our little world, we generally feel calm and can go with the flow. However, when we get the unexpected, middle-of-the-night phone call telling us to come to the hospital immediately, or we discover that a spouse has been unfaithful or that our child has been arrested, or we miscarry the baby we longed for, or we have a life-altering accident, or we are diagnosed with cancer, our easy peace dissolves into internal chaos. If our equilibrium isn't restored fairly quickly, we can become riddled with discontent. Sometimes we wonder: Does God even care about what has happened? Why does he allow bad things to happen to people who are trying to live the way he wants them to? Rationally we understand that we live in a fallen world where there's plenty of injustice, sickness, and sorrow. But sometimes we get stuck in the quagmire of self-pity, and that's when it's easy to compare our reality to the more "perfect" one of someone else. Then we're filled with the poison of envy and resentment on top of having to deal with our difficult situation. What a mess!

1. How do you define the word *contentment*? On a daily basis, what factors impact your contentment?

2. On a scale of 1 to 10 (with 10 being high), how do you rate your sense of contentment right now?

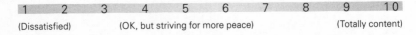

| 1 | 2 | 3 | 4 | 5 | 6 | 7 | 8 | 9 | 10 |

(Dissatisfied)          (OK, but striving for more peace)          (Totally content)

3. Gene shared his feelings about being jealous when he observed the grown son of his best friend having a "normal" life. He was happy for his friend but sad for himself. Do you ever struggle with envy, and if so, how does it affect your sense of contentment? What action steps could you take to get back on track personally and spiritually?

4. The much-loved author C. S. Lewis once said: "If I find in myself a desire which no experience in this world can satisfy, the most probable explanation is that I was made for another world."[15] What does this statement mean to you?

5. As you consider the experiences of Jason Kent in prison and Cathy Gallagher's quest for a fulfilling job, what do you think the two of them are learning about true contentment?

6. Read Philippians 4 (some verses are quoted in this chapter), and meditate on passages that are meaningful to you. Particularly pay attention to these instructions from Paul: "Don't worry about anything; instead, pray about everything. Tell God what you need, and thank him for all he has done. Then you will experience God's peace, which exceeds anything we can understand. His peace will guard your hearts and minds as you live in Christ Jesus."[16] Then write out a prayer to God, listing your worries and needs. Ask him for wisdom and peace, and invite him to guard your heart and mind this week as you intentionally practice contentment.

# CHAPTER 4

# THE SECRET POWER
# OF GRATITUDE

## SURPRISED BY THANKSGIVING

Thanksgiving puts power into living,
because it opens the generators of the heart to respond gratefully,
to receive joyfully, and to react creatively.

**C. Neil Strait**

Amid a flurry of activity in the kitchen on Thanksgiving Day afternoon, the doorbell rang. "Oh, look!" my sister, Jennie, exclaimed as she peeked out the kitchen window. "There are two of the most adorable little pilgrims at our back door. They must be selling cookies for the Girl Scouts. Will someone please open the door and let them in?" Jennie was busy getting the turkey out of the oven, while I was finishing setting the dining room table for our annual family feast.

"Aunt Carol," my nephew called, "I think you'll want to see these special visitors!"

I descended the steps leading to the back door of my sister's home and saw two little girls wearing long dresses and bonnets, looking very much like early English settlers. When they lifted their heads I couldn't believe my eyes. My two precious granddaughters, who lived in Rhode Island, stood in front of me, all decked out for the holiday in vintage outfits. It was a Thanksgiving surprise that filled my eyes with tears as the girls squealed and we shared big hugs.

"How did you get here?" I asked.

Then out of the corner of my eye I saw my son, Jason, and his lovely wife of three months. They were living in Newport where Jason was in Surface Warfare Officers School, and none of us thought he would get enough time off from his Navy training to make the long journey from the East Coast to Michigan for our Thanksgiving Day reunion. They had driven all night to make the surprise visit possible, and we were thrilled!

After hugs all around with Great-Grandpa and Grandma Afman, aunts, uncles, and cousins, another table was set up, and twenty-four family members sat down to enjoy roast turkey, mashed potatoes and gravy, green bean casserole, strawberry ice cream Jell-O, butternut squash, and sweet potato pie. After a gloriously noisy meal with children laughing and teenage cousins throwing gibes back and forth with their characteristic humor, we took a break to clear the table. Then all of us got comfortable in my sister and brother-in-law's family room, and with dessert and coffee in hand, we began our Thanksgiving tradition: a multiple-hour time of sharing what we are thankful for from the happenings of the past year, starting with the youngest child and systematically working our way up to the grandparents.

This ritual has become so meaningful that most of us think carefully in advance about what we will share. The children often shyly speak a sentence or two, but as the teens begin their annual updates, the Thanksgiving testimonies get longer and take on a serious, heartfelt tone. In past years there have been confessions, announcements, celebratory moments, and tearful tributes. This family tradition always ends with my father offering a word of thanks to God for his goodness to us during the past year. That year during my turn to speak, I expressed deep gratitude — for a new daughter-in-law; for two precocious, adorable granddaughters; and for the joy I saw on my son's face as he held his much-loved wife in his arms and responded to the spontaneous, jubilant interruptions of his new stepdaughters. Basking in the delight of that moment, I never dreamed it would be the last Thanksgiving Day I would have my son at our holiday table.

## Counting Our Blessings

In my growing-up years I had a lot to be thankful for, including a Christian home where prayers of thanksgiving to God were common. I was one of six children — five girls and one boy. (We always teased our brother because he was redheaded, freckle-faced, and born on Halloween, with a disposition to match!) Expressing praise and gratitude for my blessings was something that came naturally to me from my earliest years.

When I married Gene and five years later gave birth to a healthy son, my heart overflowed with thanksgiving. As our son grew older and eventually started junior high school, I felt like I was living on top of a mountain of blessings. I remember looking out the window one fall day and seeing a big pile of leaves that had been raked up. I knew I could never count all the leaves in that huge mound. It was a crisp, sunny day, and I spontaneously threw on a jacket, ran outside, and threw myself in the middle of the pile. Joyfully, I thought, *I am the most blessed woman alive. I have a wonderful, funny, encouraging husband, and I have a son with a compassionate heart for people and a deep love for God. I can hardly wait to see what his future holds — because it's going to be good!*

I discovered that it's easy to count your blessings and to feel thankful when positive things are happening in your life and when your family relationships and circumstances are favorable. But once Jason was incarcerated, I struggled to retain the thankful attitude that had come so easily before suffering parked itself in our lives. One of the ways the Enemy tries to erode my mental and spiritual stamina is to remind me of better days gone by, before deep pain and disappointment caught us by surprise. As I write this, we face another Thanksgiving Day, just one week away, with our son in prison. Gene jotted down his thoughts about the upcoming holiday.

Running together is a fun, male-bonding tradition in our family. For many years Jason and I ran in the Turkey Trot, a 10-K, 6.2-mile run that takes place in downtown Detroit, Michigan, just before the Thanksgiving Day parade. About five thousand runners participate in this event. My brother-in-law, Ron, and my nephews, Nathan and Jordan, regularly ran with us. They were all faster than me, but we had a grand time. We'd get up at 4:30 a.m., throw on our clothes, and drive from Port Huron to Detroit. Traditionally, we'd find an inexpensive parking place a mile or two from the start of the race. Who cared about the extra walking? Our adrenaline was flowing; we were pumped!

The weather was usually cold, often just twenty to twenty-five degrees. It was seldom raining or snowing, but it was usually windy and frigid. The experience of being in the middle of five thousand other "crazies" like us was part of the fun. Many of the runners wore ridiculous outfits. The wilder the attire, the better! Parade watchers who wanted the best seats lined the curb early. It was a party atmosphere.

The guys in our family loved this experience for many reasons — the exercise, the challenge, the upbeat atmosphere, the pride of earning the "right" to eat all we wanted at the huge Thanksgiving feast later in the day. The last race we did together was over nine years ago. Since Jason's arrest, trial, and conviction, none of us have run in the Turkey Trot again. It wasn't a conscious decision. We just didn't do it.

Last week my nephew, Jordan, called and asked if I wanted to run the race with him, his brother, and his dad this year. I was surprised by the emotion that came over me, but I said yes. When I visited Jason at the prison last week and told him about my commitment to run the race, he was energized and excited! His questions were fast and furious: When will you and Mom be leaving for the reunion? Will the race begin at the same point it did the last time we ran together? What do you think the weather will be like? Dad, do you really think you can do it? What will you eat when the race is over and you're on the way back to Aunt Jennie and Uncle

Graydon's house? You don't want to spoil your appetite for the big Thanksgiving feast!

Jason's positive attitude helped me to be thankful that God continues to encourage my son in the middle of an unlikely, unwanted, and unending life behind bars. I sometimes wonder what causes him to be so upbeat. And then I realize it's the prayers of so many people around the country who know our situation and hold my son up to the Lord.

I realized it was time for me to thank God for the large reservoir of memories my son has — of happy family reunions filled with laughter and joy and races run. I also thanked God that I can still talk to my son and spend time with him. And once again I wept for the father who lost his son at the hands of my son. All he has left of his boy are memories. I never forget that, and I often pray for him.

The hard places in our lives come in many different forms. Several years ago, I met Jill Gregory at a seminar hosted by her church. Her dynamic enthusiasm and joyful spirit captured my attention immediately. It wasn't until later that I learned about the challenges she lives with every day.

## Grateful Hearts — Jill's Story

Back-to-school shopping day had arrived for my seven-year-old, and another one of my children would be picking out her school supplies for the first time. My five-year-old daughter, Kendall, with her newly cut "bobbed" hairstyle, was thrilled that she would be going to kindergarten this fall. As I walked into Target with my four kids, Kendall ran and grabbed onto a cart for us in her eagerness. "Mom, Mom! Let's go. Come *on!*"

My oldest, going into second grade, did not share his sister's enthusiasm. As Jim picked up a pack of pencils and tossed it into the cart, Kendall literally jumped up and down in excitement as we compared which color blunt scissors we should buy. We finally decided on a pair with purple handles.

Literally hopping in the aisle, Kendall spilled her joyfulness all over us. "How many more days till school starts, Mom? I wonder who my teacher will be. Can I get this purple pencil sharpener? This is so exciting!" Then she hugged me and squeezed tightly, still jumping up and down. Her exuberance made me laugh and shake my head. I could tell it was going to be a long day as I made the rounds of school-related errands with a seven-year-old, two five-year-olds, and a three-year-old in tow.

Naturally, I was excited for my ecstatic daughter. I knew this day was coming. I had signed up Kendall for kindergarten months before. But now, standing in the school supply aisle, this rite of passage was feeling bittersweet. *I should be buying* two *of each item on our list*, I thought. In her elation, Kendall had no idea how this event was breaking my heart.

I was mourning the loss of what might have been and what will never be. When I found out I was carrying twin girls, I dreamed about what having twins would be like. My two boys are a joy, but I dreamed about the special bond that twin sisters would have, particularly because of the lifelong closeness I have enjoyed with my own two sisters. I dreamed of my twins' delight in having a built-in playmate in each other. I dreamed of them going to class together, running side by side up to the neighborhood school. I dreamed of drawings and paintings being excitedly thrust into my face and hearing all the news of what went on during the school day. Instead, Kendall would be running off to kindergarten while I held my other daughter's hand until the bus came to take her to a special-needs school another town away.

Kendall's twin, Sarah, had been diagnosed three years before with autism. Her days at school were filled with learning to speak, learning to sit in a chair during story time, and learning to use a toilet — which finally happened when she was in kindergarten. Sarah had been attending "school" since she was three in order to take advantage of an early intervention program that helped children like her.

During her first week of kindergarten, Kendall was regularly rushing home to tell me all about who she sat with, who her new friends were, and how she was already learning to read and count. I yearned to have Sarah say anything at all. In order to find out what my daughter did while she was away, I would look through Sarah's schoolbag. In the daily log kept by her teachers I would read things like, "Sarah needed help holding her crayon correctly." "Sarah is still working on drawing a straight line." "Sarah kicked the therapist five times today. We are trying to determine what may have triggered this behavior."

A few weeks into the school year, my heart sunk to a new low. Each child in Kendall's class was given an "All about Me" assignment, complete with a form to fill out and time set aside during class to share personal information with the other students. Kendall was thrilled as we filled out the survey of her favorite foods, color, flavor of ice cream, etc. I had no idea what Sarah's favorite flavor of ice cream might be. In Sarah I had a child unable to fully communicate her needs or preferences, and in Kendall I had a child brimming with eagerness to share all she thinks and feels. How I longed to have *two* jumping girls squealing in excitement.

When I picked up Kendall after school on the day of her presentation, I asked her, "So how did it go, my shining star?"

"Mom, it was so much fun!" she exclaimed. "You know, they didn't even know I was a twin. I'm the only twin in the class, but no one knew!"

"Wow, I guess not," I said, smiling at my daughter as I fought back tears. "How cool is that to be the only twin in your class?"

That night I held a pity party for myself. I cried and cried, and I reminded God that it wasn't fair. "How many people have children with no disabilities?" I railed. "How many twins are fine? Why autism? Why us? I'm tired of living with autism. I've had it! Why can't my life be like everyone else's?"

The next morning when I opened my Bible, I happened to land on a passage in the book of Job. I found humor in this "coincidence," but I also realized that my loving heavenly Father was using this particular reading to discipline me. The Lord let Job rant and get all his questions and feelings out, and then he spoke and laid down for Job the bottom line: he was God, and Job was not.

As I read about God posing his own questions to Job — about the breadth of heaven, the dimensions of space, the formation of creation, and many other things beyond human reasoning — I felt my anger, my self-pity, and my complaints about how I thought my life should be fade away. I wept and humbly agreed that I was not God and that God was in control — even when things don't go the way I want them to. After all, I reminded myself, I *knew* better. How often hadn't I seen amazing evidence of God at work in our lives!

Autism is considered a puzzle. No one is sure what causes it. Some therapies work for some and not for others, and each child's struggles are different. The common denominator among autistic children is an inability to relate normally to the world around them. When Sarah was first diagnosed, we knew we needed support. We sent out a letter and a card with a photo of Sarah to family and friends, asking for prayer. The response was amazing! Not only did loved ones respond, but also other Christians we have never met, who heard about us through the letter. As these people have faithfully prayed for us, we have witnessed doors opening for programs that Sarah needed to get into, financial provision for the many costs related to her care, and improvement in her behavior, which can be both self-destructive and violent.

Our prayer partners celebrated with us when Sarah gave her first hug and said "I love you" to my husband. This was a major accomplishment for Sarah, as most autistic children struggle with showing affection or even allowing someone to touch them. While we have constantly told Sarah throughout her life that we love her, we have often been pushed away when we've tried to hold her. The day she initiated a hug and said "I love you" was an occasion that made us practically shout for joy! Months later, when Sarah told me she loved me, I burst into tears. Talk about giving her a mixed message! I had longed to hear those words from my daughter, and while my love for her has been unconditional, it had been so hard to find ways to show love to a child who hit, screamed, and smeared her bowel movements on the walls as a way to express her anger and frustration.

This road has not been easy, and I have asked so many times for a miracle of healing in Sarah's life. But in my hardest places, where I have been broken and raw with pain, God has shown me his graciousness in ways I would not have known otherwise. My girls will start fourth grade in a couple of months, and I now have years' worth of prayer letters documenting our journey and God's faithfulness to us. Periodically I send out a newsletter with an update on Sarah, prayer requests, and stories that depict how our challenges and sorrows have been turned into experiences and lessons that have surprised and enriched us. Now I always sign each letter with what has become our family's motto: "With grateful hearts …" followed by our names.

One of our favorite verses is found in the book of Psalms: "The LORD has done great things for us and we are filled with joy."[1] Interestingly, my husband and I had this Scripture reference engraved inside our wedding bands long before this journey with Sarah began. The letters we have sent through the years are a testament of the great things God is doing and the heartfelt thanksgiving we have come to feel, even when we are between a rock and a hard place. The letters are a record of Sarah's progress, a journal of how my faith in Christ has grown, a testimony of the positive ways I have changed because of my experiences with autism, and an encouragement to me on the days I get overwhelmed. Our daughter remains autistic, yet we see the handprints of God's loving-kindness all over our lives.

Looking back on the days leading up to Kendall's entering kindergarten, I can now say I am thankful for how things worked out for my twins. Sarah's care requires a great deal of our time and energy, so school has been a place for Kendall to shine. While she was in kindergarten, she was always so proud to show me her paintings, papers, or the little bean she grew in a small cup for a science project. I am grateful I have a daughter who is able to tell me everything that happened at school. I am also grateful that Kendall is tender to her sister and loves her deeply, despite how Sarah often hits others to express her anger. There is an unmistakable bond between these sisters that is not hindered by autism.

No, this reality is not what I dreamed about for my twin girls. On some days I still grieve. Yet God knows and hears the cries of my heart. In the tight spots of my life he takes these cries and turns them to unexpected expressions of thanksgiving — and for that I am grateful.[2]

## Turning Thanksgiving into Praise

There is a fascinating story in the Old Testament about a king named Jehoshaphat. He was devoted to God and carried out a highly effective national religious education program. He is known for his multiple military victories and for developing an extensive legal structure throughout the kingdom of Judah.

The story, told in 2 Chronicles 20, begins with three allied armies declaring war on Jehoshaphat and his people. When the king is alerted that a vast army is on its way, he is shaken, and his first response is to ask for guidance from the Lord and to proclaim a fast for everyone in his kingdom. The reaction from the people is instantaneous. "The country of Judah united in seeking GOD's help — they came from all the cities of Judah to pray to GOD."[3]

King Jehoshaphat stands before them and prays powerfully: "O GOD, God of our ancestors, are you not God in heaven above and ruler of all kingdoms below? You hold all power and might in your fist — no one stands a chance against you!"[4] He goes on:

"When the worst happens — whether war or flood or disease or famine — and we take our place before this Temple (we know you are personally present in this place!) and pray out our pain and trouble, we know that you will listen and give victory … And now they've come to kick us out of the country you gave us. O dear God, won't you take care of them? We're helpless before this vandal horde ready to attack us. We don't know what to do; we're looking to you."[5]

Jahaziel, a priest who had been appointed by King David, is moved by God's Spirit to speak, and his prophetic words are powerful. "You won't have to lift a hand in this battle; just stand firm, Judah and Jerusalem, and watch GOD's saving work for you take shape. Don't be afraid, don't waver. March out boldly tomorrow — GOD is with you."[6] Jehoshaphat is so moved that he bows with his face on the ground.

The next morning the king and his forces rise early, but what Jehoshaphat instructs the people to do as they prepare for battle is totally unexpected. "Jehoshaphat appointed a choir for GOD; dressed in holy robes, they were to march ahead of the troops, singing, Give thanks to GOD, His love never quits."[7] Another translation puts it this way: "After consulting the people, the king appointed singers to walk ahead of the army, singing to the LORD and praising him for his holy splendor. This is what they sang: 'Give thanks to the Lord; his faithful love endures forever!' "[8]

Talk about a surprise! Instead of entering the battle with weapons and armor and typical frontline military personnel, Jehoshaphat instructs a choir dressed in robes to march in front of the troops, singing their thanks to God at the top of their lungs and proclaiming that his love endures forever. Their thanksgiving to God wells up in spontaneous praise, and as soon as they start shouting and voicing their gratitude to God, they get an even bigger surprise. The Lord causes the three armies coming against the army of Judah to begin fighting each other. By the time Jehoshaphat's soldiers arrive at the lookout point over the Valley of Beracah, they get the shock of their lives: the soldiers of the other armies have already killed each other! The Bible says, "Not a single one of the enemy had escaped."[9]

But the surprise isn't over yet. The story that began with threats of war and impending doom does not end in bloodshed for the kingdom of Judah. Rather, "King Jehoshaphat and his men went out to gather the plunder. They found vast amounts of equipment, clothing, and other valuables — more than they could carry. There was so much plunder that it took them three days just to collect it all!"[10] This story sounds like the plot of a spellbinding movie!

Jehoshaphat was thirty-five years old when he became king, and he ruled Jerusalem for twenty-five years. This is what was said about him: "He continued the kind of life characteristic of his father Asa — no detours, no dead-ends — pleasing GOD with his life."[11]

It would be nice to end the story right there, knowing that after the people of Judah took time for thanksgiving, proclamations of God's love, and praise, they lived happily ever after. But that's not what happened. Scripture records, "During his reign, however, he failed to remove all the pagan shrines, and the people never fully committed themselves to follow the God of their ancestors."[12] In spite of Jehoshaphat's many accomplishments, he made some wrong choices that had a far-reaching impact, primarily because he did not completely destroy idolatry in the land. I'm sure *that* biographical endnote was a surprise he didn't expect while he was reigning as a successful leader.

As I pondered the life of Jehoshaphat, I couldn't help but think of my own son. Jason definitely grew up following the godly example of his father. When training got difficult at the U.S. Naval Academy, he focused on thanking God for the opportunity to serve his country and for the privilege of becoming a military officer. He purposed to be an effective leader and a protective and godly father to his stepdaughters. He wasn't a king, but by all outward appearances he had a prosperous and respectable career ahead of him. Not unlike Jehoshaphat, however, there was a problem. Jason readily admits that he had an "idol" of his own. Rather than trust solely in God to show him a constructive and effective way to deal with his fears about his stepdaughters' safety, he became consumed with anxiety and fell back on self-reliance. The end result was deceit, death, and devastation.

## Giving Thanks No Matter What

When I was a child, my mother encouraged me to memorize Scripture. A passage etched in my mind early on was 1 Thessalonians 5:16 – 23. I think God knew how much I would need this reminder long before I was challenged to practice choosing a heart of thanksgiving in the hard places of life.

> Be cheerful no matter what; pray all the time; thank God no matter what happens. This is the way God wants you who belong to Christ Jesus to live....
>
> May God himself, the God who makes everything holy and whole, make you holy and whole, put you together — spirit, soul, and body — and keep you fit for the coming of our Master, Jesus Christ.[13]

One evening, after a long and discouraging day, I opened my e-mail and read:

*Dear Carol,*

*Recently I finished reading your books, When I Lay My Isaac Down and A New Kind of Normal. I was moved to tears and to my knees numerous times. I, too, am trying to adjust to a new normal as my chronic disease of multiple sclerosis strips me of my functions daily. I am often unable to sleep as a result and use my wakefulness as a time to pray. I am in a great deal of physical pain and find myself being directed to people who are also suffering, whether it is physical or emotional.*

*You and Gene and J.P. have been heavy on my heart each night. I just wanted you to be aware that people you don't know and will probably never meet this side of heaven are lifting you up in prayer. Thank you for being so transparent in your books. God has used them in a mighty way in my life. Thank you from the deepest part of my heart.*

*Sincerely,*
*Heidi*

I instantly realized that people like Heidi are part of an "army" of God-followers who are praying for us. I thought about the way she allows her sleeplessness and physical pain to direct her into a spiritual mind-set in which she focuses on the needs of others instead of dwelling on her own suffering.

Someone once said, "Grace isn't a little prayer you chant before receiving a meal. It's a way to live."[14] As another Thanksgiving Day approaches without my son sharing our family feast, I find myself thankful for Heidi and everyone she represents who model what it means to press into God's grace amid the obstacles their lives. I am thankful for my son's attitude of gratitude, reflected in a note to us last week.

> *My Thanksgiving Days are very different now that I'm in prison. It's easy to get depressed, and I used to go through mood swings every day — sometimes multiple times a day. But by God's grace I've become more and more stable, peace filled, and at rest in him. The best technique I have for fighting depression is making myself think of all the things I am thankful for. If I feel really bad, I make myself write those things down. I've learned how important it is to acknowledge my gratitude — either in writing or out loud to someone else — even if I don't initially believe I have anything to say. If I think and write about my blessings, I realize there's always something to be thankful for!*

This week I called my mother and told her I was deeply disappointed over a set of circumstances that filled me with anxiety and anger. She listened with compassion, as always, but I wasn't surprised by what she had to say. "Carol, have you thanked God yet? There's power in intentionally giving him praise. Taking that action will keep your heart and mind in the right place. If you choose thanksgiving over fear and resentment, you will find hidden treasure, even in this situation."

Once I followed her advice, I realized Mama was right — again! The surprising treasure in this case was that as I verbalized praise to God —

based on his character and not on the immediate circumstances causing my upset — I started to *feel* grateful. And one of the things I realized I'm most grateful for is the growing maturity I see in my son's life — for his recognition of the pain and devastation his actions brought to the family of his victim; for his ever deepening humility and understanding that he is nothing and no one apart from Christ; for his resolve not to lose a sense of purpose in his life; for his dedication to acknowledging his blessings and thanking God for them; for the way he embraces the opportunities he has to show compassion, share the grace he has been given, and extend tangible encouragement to other inmates.

More than a year ago, J.P. wrote to us about some of these realities, many of which have been a bittersweet surprise on our son's hard-fought journey toward living out his faith.

*There is a definite hierarchy in prison, which I have come to find quite ironic. Here we are, locked up in a maximum security prison, comparing ourselves with each other and measuring our "prestige" according to our reasons for being incarcerated! Some crimes are "favored" more than others by the general prison population. Thieves and murderers are at the top of the totem pole (depending on who they killed or robbed and why), and sex offenders are much lower, with pedophiles and child rapists at the bottom. Fights actually break out over who's perceived to be at the top and bottom of the pecking order of this hill. We're great at comparing our sins with everyone else's. Pathetic!*

*One of our chapel speakers reminded us recently that God looks down on us as we play "King of the Hill" on a giant manure pile, and he says, "You're missing the whole point! You all smell like crap, regardless of where you are on the pile!" (The chaplain used a more graphic word than crap!) His message hammered home how good I used to be at evaluating everyone else and justifying myself, while God's standard is perfection and we've all failed miserably. Sometimes I'm still tempted to think my acts of kindness and obedience to the Golden Rule, even in prison, earn me special favor with God, but without the right motives, everything I do that may look good to someone else is worthless—a big pile of dung.*

*The truth is, I used to be addicted to the power, knowledge, and influence I thought I had. Look where it got me! In my arrogance, mixed in a blender with self-reliance, overwhelming fear, and a mental meltdown, I killed another human being. I thought I knew so much, but I understood so little. Now I want God—and to be God's man—more than anything on earth. I'm learning to check my motives constantly, because even a spiritual discipline like Bible study, prayer, fasting, tithes/giving, or an act of service can become just another activity that I use as an end in itself rather than what it's designed for: to bring me closer to God and to prepare me to love a world in need of healing.*

*I've been fortunate in that I've gotten to know a lot of men here who have been released. I've gotten to pray with them, encourage them, challenge them, and maybe even at times mentor them a little. It's fun to be able to help people, and investing in others' lives is essential to getting the focus off myself—my own natural selfishness and ego. I find I can transcend life imprisonment a bit when I can help another man to freedom—from addictions, from selfishness, from his family legacy of abuse, from no hope of change to hope that with God living within, he can be the man he most desires to be and his family needs today.*

*Mom and Dad, I have carried burdens I wasn't meant to, but I'm realizing that not only is life all about God, but he alone will determine how mine unfolds from here. He gave me the desire to trust him to save me, the desire to make him Lord, and the strength to repent again and again. All healing is his beautiful magic working in our souls, our bodies, our minds, our spirits. I have a relationship with him today that is more personal, deep, intimate, and transparent than ever before, and I'm grateful for this. Only he can take my mess and make anything good out of it. I am just a man who has been given a lot of grace and love, who is learning little by little how to share that same grace and love with others. I'm learning to see things from the perspective of other people, and I'm slower to give advice or my opinion unless it's requested. I'm quick to empathize, pray, and love people more wisely and compassionately than ever before. I thank God that he is making these changes in my heart. This ordeal definitely has brought me closer to Jesus.*

Recently I sat with Jason in the prison visitation area, and a woman I didn't know who was visiting someone else interrupted our conversation to say, "Excuse me, but I couldn't help but overhear some of your conversation. Are you Jason Kent?" Jason nodded, indicating that was his name. She continued, "I've been told there is an inmate on this campus who is a godly man and that his name is Jason Kent. Someone told me about your mother's books too. I was hoping to meet both of you."

As we spoke with a woman we had never met before, I realized that one of my prayers for my son was being answered — that God will use him as a mighty man of valor in a very unlikely place: a maximum security prison. I felt proud of my son's emerging reputation as a man of God on the prison compound, and I voiced my thankfulness on my drive home.

*Lord, thank you for reminding me that you are not wasting my son's life. Thank you that he did not receive the death penalty for his crime. I'm grateful that he is growing in his knowledge of your truth and that he is using his leadership skills to encourage and help other inmates. Thank you for allowing Gene and me to encourage other families who are in hard places of their own. Thank you for unknown blessings already on their way. Thank you, most of all, for not forsaking us. We remain in a hard place, but we will press into you, our Rock, and find the grace we need in each moment. We are only pilgrims here on earth, and we look forward to the day when the entire family of God will surround your banquet table in heaven. Meanwhile, thank you for filling our hearts and our mouths with praise. Amen.*

## EXPLORING YOUR OWN GRACE PLACE

Most of us grew up in homes where we were taught to be courteous and polite. It was natural to say thank you when someone extended a kindness, spoke up on our behalf, or gave us a gift. However, all of us have discovered it's much more challenging to have a grateful heart when the threads of suffering weave unexpected crises into our carefully crafted designs for life. I know God is honored when we quit complaining and start thanking him in the middle of our struggles, but when faced with ongoing disappointment and loss upon loss, it's hard to remember to maintain a spirit of gratitude. I'm grateful to have a wise and godly mother, who reminds me that voicing thanks to God leads to feeling grateful — and it's hard to be in a bad mood when I have a grateful heart.

1. As you look back on your growing-up years, what are you most thankful for? What are you particularly grateful for today?

2. When you experience deep disappointment or get devastating news, which of the following reactions are you most likely to have: (1) fear; (2) anger; (3) denial? Why do you think you tend to respond in this way?

3. Review the story of King Jehoshaphat in this chapter or read it in 2 Chronicles 20:1 – 35. What were the benefits the king and his troops experienced when their first response to a negative situation was giving thanks to God? How were all the people of Judah surprised and rewarded when their leaders started what appeared to be the beginning of a battle in such an unconventional way?

4. There are many kinds of battles in our lives, and most are not in a war zone or behind prison bars. Have you ever been involved in a situation in which someone else's discipline of offering thanksgiving and praise not only broke their own chains of negativity but also liberated others in some way? Consider the impact of their decision to do so.

5. In this chapter you read the story of twin girls, Sarah and Kendall — one with autism and the other without. There are times in our lives when following the command in Scripture, "In everything give thanks,"[15] appears to be not only challenging but impossible. What did you learn from Jill's story that will help you benefit from her example?

6. This book is about leaning into "the grace place" and finding faith, safety, comfort, contentment, joy, and blessing — even when life doesn't turn out as expected. R. P. C. Hanson writes, "Grace means the free, unmerited, unexpected love of God, and all the benefits, delights, and comforts which flow from it."[16] Make a list of five ways you have experienced God's grace in the past, and then list five more ways you are discovering his grace in your current circumstances. Then choose to thank him for the specific ways he surprises you with the "benefits, delights, and comforts" of his love in the tight spots of your life.

CHAPTER 5

# UNEXPECTED KINDNESS

God will not permit any troubles to come upon us,
unless he has a specific plan by which
great blessing can come out of the difficulty.
Peter Marshall

I pulled a batch of dark clothes out of the dryer and began the mindless job of folding laundry. As I transported the piles of clean clothes to the closet, I noticed a marked change in the height of my husband's pile of black T-shirts. It was shorter than it had been in a long time — and I knew he had recently purchased more black, cotton, go-with-every-thing T-shirts.

When he arrived home I asked about the missing shirts. I noticed a fun-loving twinkle in his eyes as he said, "You'll figure it out soon. I like to surprise you." That was it. I could drag no additional information out of him.

A week later we were standing in line at the prison, waiting to go through security. Suddenly, a woman came out of the entrance to the security area sobbing. She had a sleeveless blouse on, and I overheard her say to another visitor, "I've been up most of the night and drove five and a half hours to visit my son, but the prison has changed its regulations. I'm not allowed to wear a sleeveless blouse into the visitation

107

area — and it's all I have with me. I waited in this line for two hours already, and the nearest Wal-Mart is twenty minutes away. I'm so frustrated I feel like screaming!"

My attention was captured by this unfolding drama, so I didn't even notice that Gene had slipped out of the line and walked back to our car. Moments later I saw him approach the woman — with a black T-shirt in his hand. "Ma'am," he said, "I have an extra shirt with me. It's my gift to you today. Go to the front of the line and have a great visit with your son." She thanked him profusely as she pulled on the shirt and headed into the concrete block building where she could now pass inspection.

Gene came back to me with a sheepish grin on his face. I was already smiling from ear to ear as I hugged my husband and whispered, "How long have you been passing out clothing to women you don't even know?"

"Quite a while," he said quietly. "It's my T-shirt ministry." I now understood the mystery of Gene's shorter shirt pile in the closet.

Last spring I was speaking at a women's conference in Wisconsin, and I shared the story of the disappearing T-shirts. A few weeks later, I received an e-mail from one of the attendees:

*Dear Carol,*

*I attended the retreat at Elkhart Lake. After hearing about your husband's T-shirt ministry, I wanted to help out. I would like to give you a dozen new black T-shirts to be used however you see fit. I work for JanSport, so I am able to purchase them at a good price.*

*I really enjoyed your message. What an amazing story! Who could have imagined the Lord would use your son's circumstances to help you reach out to women in all stages of their walk with God. Thank you.*

*Warmly,*
*Peggy*

The gift Peggy favored us with arrived on our front porch a week later. Gene carefully folded the T-shirts and placed them in the trunk of our car, and they have now blessed several wives and moms of inmates who were turned back in the security screening room at the prison. Peggy's gift of T-shirts through Gene's trunk distribution program reminds me that "favor" is a gift that keeps on giving. When you surprise someone with a gracious kindness, you experience the blessing of being favored yourself.

In my growing-up and young adult years, I never thought much about favor. Looking back, I'm sure I experienced it many times without giving it a second thought. It took many forms — a positive comment from a teacher on an essay, an invitation to join a group of interesting women for lunch, a husband who shows me love and respect and brings me hot coffee in bed every morning; a good education, meaningful work and ministry, enough income to pay our bills and share with others, a firstborn child — a son born in perfect health who filled my new mama's heart with joy. In retrospect, I have had a blessed life.

But what, exactly, is *favor*? As I studied this word, it intrigued me. Webster's dictionary says it is "friendly regard shown toward another, especially by a superior." It's "approving consideration or attention" or an "effort in one's behalf or interest." To me, the most surprising revelation about this unique word was that it can be "a special privilege or right granted or conceded."[1] This is the kind of favor bestowed by God. He doesn't ask us to earn extra points on "the goodness chart." He doesn't hand out merit badges. Rather, his favor is *granted*; it's a surprise blessing. It's undeserved and free! To be shown favor is to experience the smile of God through someone who graces our life with resources, approval, encouragement, opportunity, or hope when we have come upon an obstacle too overwhelming to deal with on our own. Favor is something extended to us by someone who, in some way, currently has more power and resources than we do.

You met my friend Claudine in chapter 1. Clinical depression was by no means the only challenge she has had to face in her life. Sometimes we go through multiple seasons of difficulty, and it's easy to let our pride keep us in a prison without bars because we don't like to admit we need help. After all, we have an image to uphold and we want to be looked on with respect. Claudine's authenticity reminds me to be "the real deal" and to humbly receive God's favor through the kind hands of people who genuinely care.

## Christmas, Food Stamps, and Dinty Moore Stew — Claudine's Story

I opened the refrigerator door for the third time in an hour. I think I was hoping for a miracle — that suddenly great quantities of food would magically appear. Instead I was met with the same stark reality I had seen the other two times I'd checked: one partially drunk half gallon of milk, two sticks of margarine, a Styrofoam box of leftovers from my son's dinner out with my parents the night before, and the usual assortment of condiments.

We were out of food.

Actually, we had been out of food for several days. The day before, I had spent all of five minutes going through the kitchen cabinets to see what we had left: a nearly empty box of Cheerios, two packages of dried pinto beans, one and a half loaves of bread, two cans of spinach, and one can of beets. I had discovered the beets hidden at the very back of a bottom shelf. I knew our food situation was really getting bad because canned beets, something I normally would never choose to eat, were starting to look good.

Today, as I shut the refrigerator door, I had to face reality. Not only were we very short on food, but we were also out of money. We only had the milk and Cheerios because my parents kept buying extra items when they went to the grocery store. Dad was always showing up at our door with milk, toilet paper, and paper towels. "They had it on special so I got you one too," he would say. I knew he was concerned about us and wanted to make sure that our six-year-old had milk to drink.

Now it was only nine days until Christmas. The holidays were typically a great time for me to make money on the products I marketed through my home-based business. But this year I had used all my sales proceeds to pay household bills instead of reordering new stock to sell. My husband had been on medical leave from his job for more than six months, and his company wasn't coming through with the short-term disability payments he had been promised. I had been trying for weeks to get an outside job. I had been successful in sales for years, so I assumed finding a job would be easy. It wasn't. I'd been self-employed for so long that I didn't have a work record for prospective employers to look at. No one would hire me.

Desperation was setting in. I couldn't buy food, let alone any gifts for Christmas. Standing at my kitchen sink, I stared out the window and let the tears I'd been fighting all day come out. I had to figure out something. But what?

"God, what am I supposed to do?" I cried. "We don't have money. I can't get work. We don't have food. I'm tired of mooching off my family. Show me what to do!"

No answer.

I waited.

Still no answer.

I had made a decision several years before to trust God with a major problem and to relinquish the results to him. I knew he could work miracles, easily — and I'd seen him do so before. But I'd also learned that just sitting and waiting passively wasn't usually the way to handle a crisis. I had a strong sense that God wanted me to take action as well.

I didn't care for the idea that came to me, but four hours later, I pushed open the door of the waiting area of our county Department of Human Services office. Thankfully it was located fourteen miles from my hometown. I was nervous and embarrassed. I had two dear friends and three customers who worked for the DHS. I was petrified someone would recognize me. I had dressed casually and wore no makeup. I was hoping to be incognito.

At the receptionist window I hurriedly signed my name and then almost ran to the far corner of the room. There I found a seat where my back would be to the front door. I hung my head forward so my page-boy hairstyle would hide my face. Grabbing a magazine off the table next to me, I pretended to read. For the second time that day, I could feel the tears forming in my eyes. I blinked them away.

After what seemed like hours but was probably just a few moments, I heard a woman's voice calling my name.

I jumped up and turned around. Good. I didn't know her. I glanced quickly around. Thankfully there was no one else waiting that I knew either.

As I walked toward her she smiled. "Are you Claudine?"

I answered with a barely audible yes.

"Well, Claudine, I'm Cheryl. Come on back to my office and I'll see if I can help you." She could tell I was fighting back tears.

"Are you applying for food stamps, WIC, or welfare?" she asked.

"I don't know," I stammered. "I think just food stamps."

For years when I'd see people using food stamps at the grocery store, I'd mumble under my breath, "Get a job." Now I was going to be the one they mumbled about. I was horrified.

Cheryl smiled at me as we got settled in her office. "First, why don't you tell me a little bit about your situation."

"My husband is sick and on medical leave," I started. "His company isn't paying his disability benefits. We might have to hire an attorney. I haven't been able to get the income from my business that I normally do." The more I talked the faster I went. "So I tried to get another job, but no one would hire me because I haven't worked outside of my home for a very long time. I don't want to be here today. I have friends working here. The Kennedys are my good friends, and I don't want them to see me. And I even have customers who work here, but I hardly have any product left because I used the sales money to pay bills." It all came out in a jumbled mess. I told her that no one in my family had ever used public assistance and how embarrassed I was.

Cheryl listened, wrote down a few things, and asked a few questions.

Finally she looked at me and said, "You don't need to be ashamed about this. You've paid into the system for years so others could receive help. Now it's your turn. It's OK. You are the reason this system was set up. There are a lot of people who try to abuse it. You are not one of them. We can help you until you can get back on your feet. And you *will* get back on your feet. I can tell," she added emphatically.

I filled out the papers and signed my name.

"Can you come back tomorrow?"

"I guess. Do I need to come back?"

"If you can come back tomorrow and bring your utility bills, I might be able to help you on those too. Are you behind on them?"

"Yes. We don't have a phone now — it was the easiest to let go. My electricity bill is paid up. I just have gas and water that I'm behind on now."

"Well, come back tomorrow, bring your gas and water bills, and I'll bet we can help. It will take a few days to process the food stamps. Until then, do you have any food in your house?"

"A little," I said, and I told her what I'd found during my recent inventory.

"Stay here just a minute. Let me get something, and then I'll walk out with you."

She disappeared down a hall. Five minutes later, she walked back in the room carrying two large brown paper sacks.

"Here's some food for you. We keep a pantry here so we can take care of people until their food stamps arrive. Hopefully this will be enough to tide you over."

I just stared at her. She was so nice. I don't know what I had expected — but certainly not the kindness and dignity she had heaped on me.

She carried one sack and I the other as we walked to my car.

"Before you go home I have one more thing I want you to do. Take this," she said, pressing a piece of paper into my hand. "Go to the Salvation Army here. It's on Third Street right off of Main. Give them this note. They will be able to help you with some presents for your son."

"I don't want to do that."

"It's OK. Just go. If they can't help, they will know who can. Someday you can help someone else in the same situation."

Ten minutes later, I handed a man at the Salvation Army the note from Cheryl. He opened it and read it quickly.

"Ma'am, I don't believe we are the ones who can help. You need the Lions Club in Henryetta. Do you know Bill Simmons or Donnie Smith?"

I nodded my head.

"Well, that's who you need to talk to. I'll go call them and tell them I'm sending you down there."

He left the note on the counter as he walked toward a back room where the phone was. "I'll be right back. You just sit tight."

As soon as he was out of sight I grabbed the note and read it.

"Please help this family. They have great need."

I crumbled it in my hand and hurried out the door. I was mortified. Not only did I know Bill Simmons, but Lou Ann Smith, Donnie's wife, was a friend from high school and a customer of mine. I didn't want *anyone* in Henryetta to know we were in need. I didn't want anyone to feel sorry for me. Hopefully the guy didn't remember my name.

I ran across the street to my car. I couldn't get away fast enough.

As I drove the fourteen miles home I felt a mixture of emotion. I didn't have to worry about food for a while — and that was a huge relief. But food stamps and the Salvation Army were not exactly my choice for an answer to prayer. I was horrified that my Henryetta friends had nearly found me out. I felt like the smallest thing would put me over the edge.

I turned on the radio. I had always loved Christmas. Maybe "Jingle Bells" would cheer me up. Instead Kenny Loggins began to croon, "Have yourself a merry little Christmas." That was all it took. I knew I was not going to have a Merry Christmas, and my heart was anything but light.

I lost it. Gut-wrenching sobs began to shake my body. I was crying so hard that I thought I was going to have to pull the car over and stop. Every ounce of pride I'd carried ... GONE! Every bit of denial that all of this was happening ... GONE!

I was broken. I hated the feeling.

But I did what I always do. I prayed. "God, I don't get this. I don't like this. But I love you. I trust you. I need you. Don't let me go. Overwhelm me with your presence. Teach me what you want me to learn from this. I thank you for Cheryl. I even thank you for these food stamps. Use this pain, Lord. Keep showing me that even in my brokenness, you are there. Amen."

As I prayed and cried, an amazing thing began to happen. Tears flowed out, and peace flowed in. It was as if my body was emptying out the hurt and humiliation and God was pouring something brand-new into me.

It was nearly dark when I got home. My husband and son met me at the door and carried in the sacks. We had an early Christmas that evening. I put on holiday music and turned on the tree lights while my son unpacked the groceries. There was oatmeal and orange juice that we could have for breakfast the next day. A new jar of peanut butter and another of jelly came out of a bag, along with flour, powdered milk, sugar, canned vegetables, tomato soup, canned tuna, tea, crackers, and cookies. There was cornbread mix and beans, a bag of chips and macaroni and cheese — and last, but not least, a large can of Dinty Moore stew.

I'll never forget that night. Canned stew became ambrosia as we celebrated God's meeting our needs. We laughed at how good a canned meal could be and how wonderful it was to have something beefy-tasting again. We watched a holiday movie and sang silly songs. We were a family — broken but together, sad but satisfied, unsure of our future but hopeful we'd have one.

When I went back to the DHS office the next day, I put on my best dress, my best jewelry, and my makeup. I decided that even though I didn't like food stamps, I was going to choose to see them as a positive step toward getting my confidence and self-respect back. I was going to stand up to my insecurities and fears and trust God to bring me through. And I was going to look like I felt good on the outside, even if my insides needed time to catch up.

Through my association with Cheryl, I met some new friends who eventually ended up being customers as well. My old friends, the Kennedy brothers, found out almost immediately about our needs. In fact, they invited us to attend a church Christmas party with them and their wives two days later. There they shared with us how bad they felt when they overheard Cheryl telling their supervisor, "I had this really nice lady come in whose husband hasn't been able to work for months because of health problems. She is friends with the Kennedys, and she was really embarrassed." They recognized immediately who she was talking about.

"Claudine," they scolded, "we would have helped you if we'd known. How could we be this close and not know?"

"You couldn't know because we didn't let you know. We acted like nothing new was going on. We were too proud to let you see our need."

Those four friends, already close, became our dearest confidants and champions as we dealt with Larry's illness and our legal and financial problems.

Because of our belief in the biblical principle of tithing, we made the decision to tithe on our food stamps. We received $300 per month for food, so every month I would take $30 of the food stamps and buy four-for-a-dollar canned goods, plus a few other staples, and donate them to the DHS food pantry. We had no other income coming in at the moment, and even though the public assistance wasn't technically income, it was still provision. Tithing on it was something we could do to show God our gratefulness for his faithfulness and favor.

The Kennedy brothers told me that on several occasions other DHS workers would ask, "Why does she do that? I've never heard of this." And they would get the opportunity to say, "Well, she's a Christian, and the Bible instructs Christians to tithe — to offer the firstfruits of what God is providing back to the place it came from so God can use it again." Tithing on our food stamps gave us a means to share our faith with people who wouldn't normally ask God-related questions.

Many years have passed since I stood in my kitchen weeping over nearly empty cupboards and wishing for a miracle. My refrigerator didn't magically fill with food in that moment, but God did pour out his favor on me. I had been proud and resistant to asking for help — but that didn't stop God from generously sharing his limitless bounty with me and my family. And in my brokenness I began to learn that he can take anything, even the most difficult circumstance, and make it usable. I just never thought he'd use Christmas, food stamps, and Dinty Moore stew.[2]

## Surprised by Favor

Friends like Claudine remind me that I'm not the only one whose life has taken a turn I never could have anticipated. She didn't expect to need food stamps, and I didn't expect to be the mother of an inmate. Claudine and I have had something else in common: deep need and dire circumstances that have led to an understanding of God's favor through the generosity of others. In my case, unexpected gestures of kindness have come through family members and friends who have sent gifts of food, financial support, and emotional and spiritual encouragement.

J.P. has also experienced favor, and he tells me he will never forget a time when it came from a surprising source. It all started when he was jumped by a group of inmates in county jail and beaten up pretty badly. He wrote to us about his ordeal.

*With blood dripping from my nose and my eyes, I hobbled away amidst jeers. The guards opened the electronic door remotely, and I stepped into the central hallway, leaving drops of blood as I walked. As a newbie in jail, I had foolishly assumed the corrections officers would intercede at some point, but they never did. I later learned that one of the officers actually instigated the whole thing by telling a lie to a group of inmates — he said my crime was a racially motivated execution. I didn't know when I was newly incarcerated how common it is for bored corrections officers to get prisoners worked up. Guards frequently let fights take place.*

*After being taken to the infirmary to be evaluated by the nurse on duty, I was interrogated by the officers. What remained of my pride wouldn't allow me to say who participated in the beating, assuming I could have even identified everyone involved. Next I was moved to a new cell block on our maximum security floor. I had nothing with me because all of my property was stolen after the attack. Later my Bible alone was returned to me.*

*Fortunately for me, the section of the jail I'd just been admitted to was the Christian cell block, 3B. The reason it even exists is because outside volunteers come in daily to hold Bible studies and chapel services. To be housed in this cell block, inmates have to agree to a set of guidelines — no fighting, no cussing, no stealing. And they have to attend the Bible studies and worship times.*

*I should have been happy to be there, but I was far from it. I was hurt both physically and emotionally, very angry, and devoid of trust. All the blocks were overcrowded — sometimes holding sixty-two inmates in an area designed to accommodate thirty-two — and I didn't want any more trouble. Even though the men in the Christian cell block never asked what I'd done to end up broken and bloody on their doorstep, I told them why I'd been arrested and challenged them to speak up now if they had a problem with me rather than jump on me later. They all stood mute.*

*Still wearing my bloody, dirty clothes, I looked for an open bunk. I finally found one and struggled to climb up onto it. It was at this point I realized how badly the other parts of my body hurt — from my elbows to my back to the cuts in my ears.*

*I hadn't been lying there for more than a couple of minutes when the men of 3B started to come by and introduce themselves. This kind of civility is rarely seen behind bars, but later I found it to be common among these particular guys. Later that night, I was still lying on my bed, keeping to myself. I didn't trust a single one of my cell mates, but that didn't stop them from asking me if there was anything I needed or anything they could do to help me. I remained adamant that I was fine and that I wanted no one's help.*

*But then, one by one, at least ten different guys, all ages and races, came by my rack (bed) and silently began to place items on it. I tried to protest, but I could hardly move due to pain. I watched canteen items they'd purchased individually pile up on my bunk: a toothbrush, toothpaste, soap, deodorant, a washcloth, gym shorts, a T-shirt, candy bars, paper, a pen. These items weren't provided by the jail but could be purchased from the canteen, and I knew it was a real sacrifice for the men to give to me out of what little they had.*

*I was shocked by their compassionate concern, and even more surprised by their generosity. They didn't know me and owed me nothing, yet they poured agape love all over me. I began to tear up from all the emotions within me. God used these maximum security prisoners to show me what his grace and favor looked like. I definitely didn't earn or deserve it. To be treated like this was an amazing gift that left me awed and humbled. I was more vulnerable and needy than I'd ever been in my life, and these men took care of me that night. I felt like Jesus himself was ministering to me.*

*As the months (and years) wore on, I got to know a lot of the men I originally met in 3B much better, and several friendships grew out of that night. But even more important, I became better acquainted with the source of their selflessness as my relationship with Jesus grew more intimate, personal, and concrete. I'd grown up in church and come to Christ at a young age, but my Christian cell mates modeled the truths I'd learned in Sunday school better than anyone I'd ever seen. It was one of the biggest surprises of my life.*

## A Different Kind of Inmate

Two years after moving to Port Huron, Michigan, I spent nine months taking a group of women in my Bible Study Fellowship class through the book of Genesis. I became very familiar with a Bible character named Joseph. I was fascinated by this story about a privileged son who wound up incarcerated and seemingly forgotten for two years. It seemed so unfair! That Bible study was twenty-five years ago, long before I fully understood that God uses even the most difficult experiences for good. I don't always like his methods, but I can't deny the positive results. Check out this story and decide for yourself.

Joseph was from a very large family. He was second to the youngest of twelve brothers, and he and his younger brother, Benjamin, were favored by their father. Favor can be a challenging thing when you have jealous siblings, and Joseph had lots of brothers so envious that they wanted to make his life miserable.

Joseph's family was wealthy, and he grew up with servants, large flocks of sheep and goats, herds of cattle, and camels. But despite being blessed with financial resources, this large family experienced some deep-rooted misery. The Bible states, "Jacob loved Joseph more than any of his other children because Joseph had been born to him in his old age. So one day Jacob had a special gift made for Joseph — a beautiful robe. But his brothers hated Joseph because their father loved him more than the rest of them. They couldn't say a kind word to him."[3] (If you grew up as the oldest child in your family and watched a younger sibling have fewer rules, more freedom, and special favor in the form of gifts, approval, or personal liberty, I know you identify with this story!) Also unique to Joseph was his ability to foretell the future through dreams. He may have been a bit unwise with the way he flaunted that ability in front of his older brothers, and in addition to the paternal favoritism, the result was family conflict.

One day Joseph's older brothers were out of town, and his father asked him to go check on his siblings and their flock. By the time Joseph arrived, his brothers had already traveled twenty more miles to another city. As Joseph made the last leg of the journey, he was spotted by his brothers, and one of them yelled out: "Here comes that dreamer!"[4] His siblings "greeted" him by taking his colorful coat and throwing him into that not-so-lovely "Sheraton on the Plains" — an underground cistern. The brothers had a meal together while Joseph remained in the pit.

Along came some traders, complete with camels, and Joseph's brothers sold him as a slave for twenty pieces of silver. The brothers then dipped Joseph's coat in goat's blood and sent it back to their father to make him think that Joseph had been eaten by a wild animal. (And I thought some members of *my* family were strange!)

What happens next is an intriguing tale that weaves threads of suffering, favor, and blessing together in an unlikely cord of three strands. Consider how Joseph's life unfolded after his brothers did him wrong.

Joseph was an unpaid servant, but because of God's favor, he became Potiphar's personal assistant and was put in charge of the household affairs and property management.[5]

Potiphar's wife found Joseph attractive, and her first recorded words to him are, "Lie with me."[6] (That direct approach left no room for guessing games about her desired result — sleeping with the head slave!)

Joseph resisted her advances, but Mrs. Potiphar told her husband that Joseph tried to defile her. The favored servant was thrown in prison, seemingly forgotten, for two years.

As the mother of an inmate who is striving to live for God in a maximum security prison, this description of what happened next takes my breath away because it reminds me that the key to favor is *God's presence* in the middle of our circumstances.

> But the LORD was with Joseph in the prison and showed him his faithful love. And the LORD made Joseph a favorite with the prison warden. Before long, the warden put Joseph in charge of all the other prisoners and over everything that happened in the prison. The warden had no more worries, because Joseph took care of everything. The LORD was with him and caused everything he did to succeed.[7]

Then Pharaoh's head cupbearer and his baker fell out of the graces of their leader and were thrown into the same prison with Joseph. Both of these men had separate, unsettling dreams, and Joseph was able to accurately interpret those dreams. Within a short time, the dreams came true. The cupbearer was restored to his original position, but the baker was beheaded and impaled on a post. (Ugh!) The cupbearer didn't tell Pharaoh about Joseph's help in prison until two years later when the king had a dream he didn't understand. That's when the cupbearer remembered the interpretation Joseph had given him of his own dream and recommended Joseph to the king.

Pharaoh summoned Joseph from prison and requested his help. Joseph's response reveals a lot about his humble, God-reliant spirit: "It is beyond my power to do this…. But God can tell you what it means and set you at ease."[8] Pharaoh describes his wildly puzzling dreams about seven fat cows walking up out of the river, followed by seven sick-looking, scrawny cows coming out of the Nile and standing beside the well-nourished cows. Joseph immediately interprets the dreams, telling Pharaoh that both dreams mean the same thing: God is instructing Pharaoh in advance about what he is to do because there will be seven years of plenty in the land, followed by seven years of famine. Joseph continues with the interpretation by encouraging Pharaoh to find an intelligent and wise man to put in charge of the entire land of Egypt and to appoint supervisors to oversee the gathering and storing of one-fifth of all of the crops during the prosperous years so there will be food for the people during the seven years of devastating famine that will follow.

Suddenly, unexpected favor is lavished on Joseph by Pharaoh.

So Pharaoh said to Joseph, "You're the man for us. God has given you the inside story — no one is as qualified as you in experience and wisdom. From now on, you're in charge of my affairs; all my people will report to you. Only as king will I be over you."

So Pharaoh commissioned Joseph: "I'm putting you in charge of the entire country of Egypt." Then Pharaoh removed his signet ring from his finger and slipped it on Joseph's hand. He outfitted him in robes of the best linen and put a gold chain around his neck. He put the second-in-command chariot at his disposal, and as he rode people shouted "Bravo!"

Joseph was in charge of the entire country of Egypt.[9]

What followed is a remarkable story that reminds all of us that when we are in difficult circumstances (as Joseph was in prison), God is often preparing us for a major work — perhaps to do something greater than we ever would have accomplished if life was easier. Joseph orchestrated the gathering and storing of so much grain during the seven years of plenty that the quantity was uncountable. He married and had two sons, and once again we see God's favor: "Joseph named the firstborn Manasseh (Forget), saying, 'God made me forget all my hardships and my parental home.' He named his second son Ephraim (Double Prosperity), saying, 'God has prospered me in the land of my sorrow.' "[10]

Talk about experiencing favor! Joseph was able to forget hardships like being sold into slavery by his brothers and being thrown into prison without just cause. And then he experienced the double blessing of prospering in the land where he had experienced so much sorrow. What a life! What a story!

And it gets even better. When the famine came, Joseph's cruel brothers needed food for themselves and for their families. They came to him and begged for mercy, pleading to be Joseph's slaves. "But Joseph replied, 'Don't be afraid of me. Am I God, that I can punish you? You intended to harm me, but God intended it all for good. He brought me to this position so I could save the lives of many people.' "[11]

In the end, because of the favor Joseph experienced from God through Pharaoh, kindness was extended to Joseph's father and to his brothers and their families. They were allowed to move to the best part of the land. Joseph treated his brothers with surprising kindness because he recognized the powerful way in which God works all things for good. Joseph ended with these words of assurance to his brothers: " 'No, don't be afraid. I will continue to take care of you and your children.' So he reassured them by speaking kindly to them."[12] Favor doesn't get much better than that!

## Favor Multiplies

As our family is living out a reality far different from what we once dreamed, God has repeatedly reminded us of his favor in the middle of difficulties. My son is not Joseph; he was found guilty of his crime. Nevertheless, we are experiencing double portion blessings in the land of our suffering that are greater than we might ever have experienced if life had been easier.

What are these blessings? The joy of spending time talking to the child of an inmate as I wait in a long line to go through prison security. Instant compassion for hurting people. Listening to the needs of others instead of obsessing about my own heartache. Ministry opportunities for Jason behind bars. Challenging people to get involved in prison ministry by visiting an inmate or collecting games and coloring books for the visitation area. A sense of the shortness of life compared to the length of eternity.

As the years go by, I am more aware of what a brief time all of us spend on this earth. I recently met a woman who told me her brother was in prison with a life sentence. She was struggling emotionally with the "forever" aspect of his incarceration, but one night she had a dream. Jesus had returned for his own, and just as she was about to enter heaven, she saw a group of men in prison garb, with their hands in shackles and their feet in leg irons. Just as they got to the gates of heaven, all of the manacles fell off, and the former prisoners were shouting for joy because they were finally *home*, and they were walking in freedom. Theologically speaking, I don't know the exact time when prisoners will be free of their restraints and at home with the Lord, but this kind stranger's story blessed me by reminding me that whether Jason walks in freedom in this lifetime or in the next, he will one day be free indeed — and it won't be long!

Mother's Day has been hard for me since Jason's arrest. A couple of years ago, my nephew called and said, "Happy Mother's Day, Aunt Carol." He was full of news of what was happening in his university classes and the new friends he was meeting. After we said good-bye, I realized he had surprised me with the call on Mother's Day because he knew I'd be lonely and sad with my son in prison. He never spoke those words, but I felt the kindness of his tender concern with the timing of his call.

Most precious to me was a conversation I recently had with my mother. "Carol Joy," she said, "since you were a little girl I have been blessed to be your mama. I love you more than words can express. You have always been a bright light in my life. It hurts me so much that you have such a heavy burden to carry because I know you love your son as much as I love you." I thanked Mama and realized how favored I am to have such a rich heritage of faith and love. Being loved deeply has filled me with love to give to others.

Favor and kindness are gifts that keep multiplying because as fast as we splash favor on others, our own supply is replenished in surprising ways. The famous aviator Amelia Earhart said, "No kind action ever stops with itself. One kind action leads to another. Good example is followed. A single act of kindness throws out roots in all directions, and the roots spring up and make new trees. The greatest work that kindness does to others is that it makes them kind themselves."[13]

When I wrote *When I Lay My Isaac Down*, my first book about our journey with our son, I told the story of struggling with depression for the first time in my life. One afternoon my doorbell rang, and the florist delivered an exquisite bouquet of one dozen long-stemmed yellow roses. The note read:

*Dear Carol,*

*You once gave us some decorating advice that was very helpful. You said, "Yellow flowers will brighten any room." We thought you could use a little yellow in your life right now.*

> *Love,*
> *Bonnie & Joy[14]*

Over the years since that book was written, "yellow favor" has been showered on me many times over. Linda, a friend from Canada, still sends me cards in yellow envelopes. One of my sisters always wraps my birthday gifts in yellow paper. A retreat group in Texas made yellow T-shirts for their participants the year I spoke. Yellow flowers periodically show up at my door — sometimes from a total stranger with a note saying, "I'm praying for your family today." Many people who have read that book tell me they regularly send yellow roses to people who need to feel God's comfort in their hard places.

The stories of black T-shirts, Dinty Moore stew, Jacob's brothers, the inmates in cell block 3B, and yellow roses express a simple but powerful truth: favor multiplies as it is given away.

## EXPLORING YOUR OWN GRACE PLACES

Favor is something most of us longed for from parents or teachers while we were growing up. We enjoyed receiving it — especially when it came in the form of a surprise blessing. Someone went to bat for us, gave us a tangible gift that met a need, or offered us an opportunity for advancement. If we're honest, we'll admit that we appreciate being favored as adults just as we did when we were kids. To have someone go out of his or her way to support us lifts our spirits and makes us feel valued.

1. Identify a person in your past or present who has favored you at a time when you didn't expect it. What did he or she do, and how did the caring gesture(s) impact your life?

2. By its nature, favor isn't earned — it's a free gift. It doesn't require a timely payback plan or an "I owe you." In your spiritual life, how have you experienced this kind of favor from God?

3. As you consider the story of Joseph and the dynamics in his family, reflect on your own relationships. Have you experienced how the wrong kind of favoritism can cause jealousy and tension in a family, work, or ministry situation? What are some practical steps for avoiding this negative form of favor?

4. When Joseph's brothers sold him into slavery, they never dreamed they would need his mercy and help someday. Have you ever extended favor to someone who was unkind to you in the past? If so, what happened, and how did it impact you and the person who received grace from you?

5. The dictionary contains many definitions of *favor*. Which of the following forms of favor is easiest for you to practice? Why?

    ✦ To assist an individual who needs tangible help with goods or services

    ✦ To support a worthy cause

    ✦ To give affirmation to someone who is struggling with self-esteem or self-respect

6. Today God continues to favor us with his Word — his written letter to us. This week write a letter to someone who favored you in the past with kind words, personal support, or tangible resources. Let that person know how their unexpected favor made a difference in your life. Then think of one person who isn't expecting your assistance right now, and do one thing to help. Remember, it can be as simple as sharing a can of Dinty Moore stew!

# CHAPTER 6

# WHY DO YOU WEEP?

## SURPRISED BY JOY

*I've survived because I've discovered a new and different
kind of joy that I never knew existed—a joy that can coexist
with uncertainty and doubt, pain, confusion, and ambiguity.*
Tim Hansel

Gene and I dropped into bed, exhausted. It had been a fast-paced, fun day as we took care of last-minute details for Jason's wedding and worked on programs for the reception. It was September 1998, and in just a few days our son and his bride would be repeating their vows in front of family and friends in our then-hometown of Port Huron, Michigan.

Before dozing off, I heard the faint strains of a romantic love song coming from the sound system in the family room. Wondering who was still awake, I cracked open the door and saw my son and his bride-to-be in each other's arms, dancing around the room, with only the light of the moon shining in through the wall-sized windows that faced the St. Clair River. They held each other closely and I briefly took in the blissful expression of joy we sometimes describe as "young and in love."

Smiling, I closed the door and climbed back into bed. Moments later, surprising sounds reverberated through the walls. I heard giggling, squealing, running, falling, more laughter, and outbursts of childlike abandon, complete with unrestrained shrieks. This time I threw on my robe and headed toward the commotion. There they were — J.P. and his fiancée, chasing and tickling each other, unfettered and unaware of anything but the sheer delight of enjoying each other.

That perfect picture of consummate joy will forever remain etched in my mind. My mother heart needed to see my son so undeniably happy and totally in love with the woman he was about to marry. She made his joy complete. At the time I thought their happiness together would last forever.

Fast-forward nine years to what had become a typical Sunday night for Gene and me. We had flown back to Florida following a speaking engagement in Louisiana. After driving the forty miles to Lakeland from the Tampa airport, Gene dropped me off at the mailbox before driving the car up a short hill and into the garage. I pulled a myriad of letters, catalogs, shopping flyers, and bills out of the overstuffed box before picking up the newspapers that had gathered at the end of our driveway during our brief time away.

Once inside the house, I scanned the envelopes, quickly sorting the urgent and important pieces from the junk mail. On top of the "important" pile was an envelope addressed to me in my son's handwriting, much like his father's in shape and appearance. I always experienced joy when a letter from Jason arrived.

Eagerly opening the letter, I wasn't prepared for what I was about to read.

> *Dear Mom,*
>
> *If people could visit me in cell block C3, the first thing they would notice is the noise. But a close second would be the smell of old mold, followed by sweat, cigarette smoke, bad breath, funky feet, body odor, urine, new mold, and fear.*

Immediately I started to feel queasy. I found myself wondering how the smell of *old* mold and *new* mold differ. I quickly realized I had trouble with even one of those aromas, and I felt momentarily nause-ated at the thought of so many repulsive odors in combination. And I had never considered the possibility that *fear* had a scent.

*Back to the noise. Whether it's the rumble of fifty men all talking at once, the screams of men playing card games won and lost, or the applause for athletes on television, it's incessant. Structurally, prison is full of metal-reinforced concrete, lots of steel — beds, doors, foot lockers, window frames — and Lexan. Real glass and Plexiglas are deemed too dangerous. Each building is like a superstrong, hurricane-proof fortress, but it's not designed to protect us from the weather; it's there to protect the world from us. This distinction is never forgotten.*

*Right now, fifty-six men share a common room with one television where we are supposed to vote on what programs to watch. However, democracy is rarely practiced. Fights regularly erupt over the selection of television programs — with major disagreements about whether to watch a mindless sitcom, a children's cartoon show, or a news program.*

*One of the first skills I had to learn after being sentenced to prison was to zone out the cacophony as best I could in order to concentrate enough to read, write, study, or pray. If I allowed myself to dwell on the banging, drumming, pounding, or crashing, I quickly became bitter or angry, unable to do much else but seek to vent my frustration on those around me.*

*Mom, some days I sit in this hellhole and am tormented by snapshots in my mind — particularly of my girls, whose presence I long for every day. In my memory I see them dancing in time to the music on the radio. They twirl, jump, spin, and look at me with laughter in their eyes. They hunger for my approval, and I love to affirm them. They love to put on a show, and I'm amazed at the grace of their movements and their tender hearts toward me as they perform. I feel an awesome responsibility in being a daddy, loving them well, and raising them to be godly women.*

*They loved to play dress-up with anything they could find as a prop. One day our six-year-old walked into the room wearing my khaki Navy officer's shirt with my warfare pin, ribbon, and rank in place. The shirt came all the way down to her shins. She was also wearing my khaki pants, holding them up at the waist with her tiny hands. She shuffled forward in my black leather shoes, with a good four inches to spare in the heels. She topped off her new look with my garrison cover on her head. She raised her hand for a quick salute, then grabbed her pants before they fell down while loudly proclaiming, "I'm in the Navy, just like Daddy!"*

*She was all smiles as she shuffled along amidst our laughter. I felt a joy I'd never known before. She was just playing dress-up, but I powerfully understood the trust she had in me to protect her from all harm and knew inside that I'd never leave her hope in me disappointed.*

By nature I'm an upbeat person, and I like to "forget" the realities of prison life. While I long to know how my son is doing and what challenges he is facing, reading this letter about J.P.'s "new normal," as well as his heartfelt recollections, was causing my mother heart to ache at a whole new level.

From the depths of my being, I cried, *Lord, how is it possible that everything in our lives has changed in such an unimaginable way? How could all that joy my boy and his family were experiencing have gone up in smoke? He thought he was experiencing a joy that would last indefinitely. O God, how could it all have turned upside down?*

There was more of the letter left to read, but I had to put it aside for a while and just let the tears come. Again.

## Joy Is Not the Absence of Sorrow

Helen Keller, blind from the age of nineteen months, once said, "We could never learn to be brave and patient, if there were only joy in the world."[1] I have come to understand what she meant. Sometimes the absence of joy helps us to understand and appreciate what it really is.

Mary Magdalene knew much about sorrow. Her life, as recorded in the New Testament, reads like a modern-day soap opera! But because of Jesus she also learned much about joy. Mary Magdalene's life had been intolerable before she met Jesus. Her first surprise in her relationship with him came when he freed her from demonic bondage that had filled her with fear, emptiness, and frustration.[2] She is sometimes mistakenly characterized as a prostitute in popular stage productions and movies, but the Bible says only that she was possessed by seven demons, from which Jesus delivered her. This encounter with him gave her a whole new beginning; her mental, physical, and spiritual imprisonment became a thing of the past. She immediately understood the value and the power of staying close to Jesus. She owed him everything!

Mary Magdalene's next surprise was the joy of being part of the team of people who served Jesus during his public ministry.[3] After Jesus delivered her from her bondage, she followed him from town to town across Galilee and Judea, helping to provide for him out of her minimal resources. She no doubt enjoyed the kind eyes and the approving smile that flashed across his face whenever he looked in her direction. Mary Magdalene, formerly an odd woman with demon-possession, was now among Jesus' band of followers. Talk about the road trip of all road trips!

During the summers between two of my university years I traveled with a talented musical team. Our director booked us to do concerts in churches and community centers and at outdoor festivals and art fairs, and for eight weeks we "hit the road" together. We ate all our meals together, laughed at each other's jokes and antics, and bonded. Lifetime friendships were forged because our road trips produced an intimacy that deepened quickly.

I've tried to imagine what it must have been like for Mary Magdalene to be part of the team that went everywhere with Jesus — watching him perform miracles, eating together, listening as he taught, observing the grace he poured out on people who needed hope, healing, and faith. For Mary Magdalene to have the privilege of being included in that close circle of people who accompanied Jesus during the three years of his public ministry had to mean she experienced acceptance, intimacy, trust, and love. She found "the grace place," for sure. "How could Mary not love such a man?" authors Ann Spangler and Jean Syswerda write. "How could she not want to do everything for him?... to be close to Jesus; to witness healing after healing; to be stirred, surprised, and refreshed by his teaching. This, indeed, was joy to a woman unaccustomed to joy."[4]

Jesus had plenty of followers when there was free bread and when he performed dramatic miracles. However, when the journey became tough and his teachings were hard to understand, many turned their backs and no longer followed him. But Mary Magdalene would not walk away. In fact, her commitment to her Lord was never more evident than at the cross. All four of the gospel writers indicate she was there. John recounts: "Jesus' mother, his aunt, Mary the wife of Clopas, and Mary Magdalene stood at the foot of the cross."[5] (I love stick-like-glue friends and family! During the agonizing five days of Jason's trial, our family members took time off work, used personal funds to travel to Florida, and sat through endless hours in the courtroom, waiting with us, holding us, weeping with us. They served us by being there for us, the way Mary Magdalene was for Jesus.)

The drama that follows in John 20 is heart-stopping! To be an eye-witness to the crucifixion of a dear friend would be more than I could bear — the bloody body, bruised and beaten, carrying every disgusting sin humankind would ever commit. To see him tortured and unfairly judged as a criminal. To hear the pounding of the nails as they tore through his flesh and anchored him to the wood of the cross. To see the soldiers gambling for his clothing. To hear the guttural groaning as he spoke: "My God, my God, why have you abandoned me?"[6] To witness the sky turn black for three hours. Looking only at the facts, this horrific event depicts the antithesis of joy.

But Mary Magdalene didn't leave. Mark records that when Joseph of Arimathea took Jesus down from the cross and laid him in a tomb, "Mary Magdalene and Mary the mother of Joseph saw where Jesus' body was laid."[7] The next morning, Mary returned to the tomb to anoint Jesus' body, but by the time she got there, she was stunned to see that the stone that sealed the tomb had been rolled away. Immediately she went to Peter and John and blurted out her worst fears: "They took the Master from the tomb. We don't know where they've put him."[8]

The disciples ran to the tomb and looked for themselves. When they discovered that Jesus was missing, they went back home. But not Mary Magdalene. She did what I do when I'm sad, confused, helpless, and hurting. She had a good cry. "But Mary stood outside the tomb weeping. As she wept, she knelt to look into the tomb."[9]

All of us have had "empty tomb" moments. We assume that the worst-case scenario has happened. Our dreams are dashed. A friend betrays us. We sob over lost opportunities. Our financial stability crumbles. A loved one dies after we've prayed for healing. Our son gets a life-without-the-possibility-of-parole sentence. In an empty-tomb moment, it appears that the living God has left our life and is nowhere to be found. We are sure no good thing will come out of our situation, and there is nothing more distressing than not being able to find him in the middle of our dilemma.

Mary Magdalene's problem, and my problem too, is that we don't always recognize the empty-tomb *reality*. When Mary Magdalene actually looked into the tomb, something amazing took place: she "saw two angels sitting there, dressed in white, one at the head, the other at the foot of where Jesus' body had been laid." That had to be a shock! "They said to her, "Woman, why do you weep?"

"They took my Master," she said, "and I don't know where they put him."[10]

Then she turned away and saw Jesus but didn't recognize him. She assumed he was the gardener. "Jesus spoke to her, 'Woman, why do you weep? Who are you looking for?' "[11]

Mary Magdalene's response is predictable: "Mister, if you took him, tell me where you put him so I can care for him."[12]

Then Jesus speaks her name: "Mary."[13]

She instantly recognizes the sound of his voice.

Turning to face him, she said in Hebrew, "*Rabboni!*" meaning "Teacher!"

Jesus said, "Don't cling to me, for I have not yet ascended to the Father. Go to my brothers and tell them, 'I ascend to my Father and your Father, my God and your God.'"

Mary Magdalene went, telling the news to the disciples: "I saw the Master!" And she told them everything he said to her.[14]

Mary Magdalene was graced by a huge surprise: The risen Christ appeared to *her* before anyone else. What a joy-filled moment! Her Lord was *alive*! But beyond that, Jesus honored Mary Magdalene by appearing *first* to her — at a time in history when women weren't even considered legitimate witnesses. Matthew's account of the scene says that Jesus appeared to "the other Mary" in addition to Mary Magdalene.[15] The fact that he chose women to show himself to and gave them such amazing and joyful news to carry back to the disciples is, as always, "just like Jesus" in terms of how his entire life and way of operating was a surprise to everyone in his day. A glorious, joyful surprise!

Ken Gire writes, "In his triumph, Jesus could have paraded through the streets of Jerusalem. He could have knocked on Pilate's door. He could have confronted the high priest. But the first person our resurrected Lord appears to is a woman without hope. And the first words he speaks are, 'Why are you crying?'"[16]

I love that Jesus didn't say, "It's me, you idiot. Don't you recognize me? Why are you whimpering and getting so emotional? Get a grip!" The fact that Jesus recognized the genuine heartache of a woman who was sobbing tells me that he cares about my tears too. And that thought fills me with joy because I've cried a lot. I know my tears matter to him.

"Life need not be easy to be joyful," said William Vander Hoven. "Joy is not the absence of trouble but the presence of Christ."[17] Mary Magdalene came to understand this truth intimately. And in her own way, so did one of my lifelong friends, Diana Pintar. In a moment when she felt an overwhelming sense of loss, God took some of the sting out of the experience by granting her a brilliant flash of joy.

## Woody's Homecoming — Diana's Story

It had been a difficult, emotional day. It was one among many difficult days since my dad had been diagnosed with stage-four lung cancer.

The hospice aide had come that morning. Tender yet proficient, she bathed and shaved Dad. We chuckled while we watched him comically contort his face to accommodate the razor. She brushed his teeth. He sighed in appreciation. Lung cancer had beaten his body, but it had not defeated his sweet spirit.

The hospice nurse came next. "His heartbeat is irregular," Janeane said. "It could be today; it could be tomorrow." Her voice trailed off. "You know Woody; he will do it in his own way, at his own time."

We nodded in understanding. The remainder of the day was tense with anticipation.

When the large grandfather clock in the front hallway chimed 8:00 p.m., my sister Julie and I rose in unison to perform the familiar evening routine. I held Dad's blanket and rolled him on his side while Julie repositioned the pillow under his hips to try to prevent bedsores. Then, Julie measured out Dad's evening medication while I held the water glass. Dad obediently swallowed one large pill after another. Before we left the room, I leaned over, as always, and kissed his broad, smooth forehead.

Afterward, we joined the rest of the family in the living room. The conversation was hushed, frequently lapsing into long silences. Above the quiet was the incessant ticking of the grandfather clock. It counted off the seconds with great authority. Across the hall, Mom kept vigil beside Dad's bed. It was the first time she had been alone with him all day.

I think Dad chose that private moment, that intimate time when he was finally alone with his wife, to say good-bye to his beloved bride of sixty years in his own tender way. At the same time, after months of a long and painful struggle with cancer, he said good-bye to this earthly life.

We looked up with apprehension when Mom appeared at the living room door. "I think he's gone," she said quietly. I glanced at the grandfather clock. It was 8:20.

Speechless, we filed into the bedroom. It seemed as if nothing had changed. I was startled to see that Dad looked just like Dad. I expected that death would change him somehow. Yet here he was — lying in bed, just as I'd left him. His breathing had stopped, but he was still my daddy.

Then, in an instant, I realized he was not. My father was gone. He was gone!

Suddenly, an intense, deep, overwhelming longing consumed me. I was a grieving child who hungered to hear my daddy's voice, to feel my daddy's touch, to know my daddy would always be there when I needed him. At the same time, I knew that none of those things would ever be again. The part of my heart that belonged to my father broke. It seemed that, by dying, he had ripped away a piece of my very being.

Grief knifed though my soul. Isolated in my emotional agony, and only vaguely aware of the others in the room, I caressed my father's face. I kissed his forehead, tears cascading down my cheeks. My knees buckled under the weight of my sorrow.

Finally, kneeling beside the bed, forehead pressed against the floor, I sobbed quietly, "Oh God! Oh God!" I felt like this loss had suddenly and permanently changed me, making me less than I had been before. Fear joined grief. I wasn't at all sure how I was going to make it through this.

But I was about to be reminded that God offers amazing reassurance for moments exactly like these. He promises that even when we walk through the valley of the shadow of death, we need not be afraid, because he is present with us.[18] He says that in his presence we can experience "fullness of joy."[19] At the hour of my father's death, God was present. Joy was coming.

When I rose to my feet, I saw Dad's prayer shawl folded at the end of the bed. At the onset of his illness, when I began my role as caregiver, I "knit and prayed" through autumn while my mother and I waited in hospital waiting rooms as Dad fought for his life against the malignant cells that were destroying his body. Working on the shawl provided not only visual encouragement for my father, who could "see" me praying for him, but also a concrete way for me to focus on prayer instead of worry and sadness.

As winter descended on Michigan, Dad grew thinner and less able to warm himself. The finished shawl, soft blue chenille draped over Dad's shoulders, was a tangible symbol of my many prayers during that season. Now, at the hour of his death, it seemed appropriate to cover him, one final time, with the shawl — and symbolically with my prayers.

I tenderly smoothed the familiar blue mantle across his lifeless form. I leaned over and kissed him on his forehead. "I love you, Daddy!" I whispered. "Go with God."

Then, suddenly, there was joy. Joy!

In such a moment, everything is brilliantly illuminated. It's like someone has taken a picture with an old-fashioned flash camera in a dark room. For an instant, it is as if an intensely dazzling light has revealed, with blazing clarity, a reality and beauty previously shrouded in darkness. Just as quickly as it comes, the illuminated moment is over. But that flash of joy is like a snapshot of what is true in the midst of our gloom and confusion. It gives us a glimpse of something so wonderful, so beautiful, so amazing, that it enlarges our souls, builds our faith, and keeps us hanging on and hoping for more. The beauty of the truth of that moment etches itself indelibly into our memory. If we are wise, we will treasure it like an exquisitely framed masterpiece in a museum. We will store it in our heart and revisit it frequently. A joyful moment is meant to be remembered and rejoiced over, again and again.

True joy happens when the Light of the world, Jesus, steps into our reality and whispers to our heart, "I am here." His very presence illuminates the moments of our lives, whether they are the desperate moments or the ordinary ones. He says, "Let me show you the truth." As the apostle Paul prayed, "the eyes of our hearts" are enlightened,[20] and we know that what we see in our circumstance is not all there is. There is so much more. There is life. There is abundant life! There is eternal life! When we experience his life within us as our present-tense reality, there is joy!

That is how it was when God surprised me by joy at my father's deathbed. In an instant, it was as if God turned on the light and gave me clear vision of what was occurring for my dad in the moment he exited this world and entered the next. I knew he was having a face-to-face encounter with the person of Jesus Christ. I knew he was experiencing joy and awe and worship beyond anything my finite mind could comprehend. Thoughts of the glad reunion that was occurring in the very moment I "lost" my father brought a smile to my heart. Dad was reuniting with loved ones who had gone before, and I could almost feel the joy of their gathering to welcome him home.

An amazing wave of relief swept over me as I understood that the cares of this world were now far behind Dad. His illness was over! There would be no more pain or suffering, no more sorrow or fear for him. Dad and I had many conversations throughout his illness, speculating about heaven and what it might be like. Dad was now experiencing the truth of it. Suddenly I understood that in all of our imaginings, we were nowhere near the half of it.

One more time I leaned over my father and whispered, "I'll bet you're surprised, Daddy. I'll bet heaven is a lot more wonderful than you ever dreamed it would be." My heart was exploding with the joy of that thought. It was only a "flash" of understanding, but what I saw with the "eyes of my heart" gave me (and still gives me) peace that passes understanding, living hope, and unspeakable joy.

On those days when I am missing my father, I have a choice. I can crawl into a black hole, pull a blanket over my head, and hide in the darkness of depression — or I can stroll through the gallery in my heart and pause for a while before the beautifully framed Masterpiece (truly the Master's handiwork!) titled "Woody's Homecoming." There, I rejoice.[21]

## The Empty Tomb Reality

My heart rejoices for Diana while at the same time I sense her deep loss. She has been a faithful friend who has had more than her share of personal challenges, disappointing relationships, and roadblocks interrupting her dreams.

One day when I was grieving my own losses after J.P.'s arrest, a package arrived in the mail. It had Diana's return address on it. Opening the padded envelope, I discovered a pewter figurine. It was the form of a child pressing his entire body into a large hand that was big enough to provide shelter and comfort. The thumb of the hand touched the child's eyes, as if to say, "Why do you weep? I am here."

Diana's note told me that during her most painful personal experience (a failed marriage and a devastating financial situation) she held on to that figurine because it reminded her of God's faithfulness in those times when she couldn't find her faith or her joy. She "just knew" it was what I needed. It has been a powerful reminder that when I am in the middle of my empty-tomb moments, when I can't find God where I think he should be, I need to press into the Rock and discover an empty-tomb reality: the surprise of his presence.

I am coming to understand a deeper meaning of the word *joy*. It's experiencing God's peace in the middle of impossible circumstances and sensing his care when life is anything but fun. It's discovering that we can delight in what he is doing in the middle of formidable obstacles. It's experiencing internal security because we are not alone. It's celebrating his powerful hand at work even when we don't understand why he allows certain things to happen. A word sometimes substituted for *joy* is *happiness*, which connotes the idea of "well-being and contentment."[22] That is the kind of joy I'm beginning to experience, and I'm realizing that Jason is learning a new definition of joy too.

After I'd had a good cry over the first part of my son's letter, I finished reading it and was surprised by joy. Once again I was struck by his growing maturity — which includes an ability to recognize joy as the presence of Christ in surprising places and in unlikely people.

*Prison is a place few of us would really call "home," unless we are making a sarcastic joke. Yet, in this very place I've seen God show up in unexpected ways, where few would expect him to visit. The greatest surprise and joy to me here is when God's presence is demonstrated in the life of another human being.*

*Sometimes I see him in a tough, violent, streetwise prisoner who has recently experienced Christ as his personal Savior, but he's still figuring out how to process what's happened to him as he talks some inmates out of beating up a convicted sex offender. Men who are in prison for committing crimes against children are hated inside the razor wire.*

*I find joy in seeing a former addict who unexpectedly finds the strength to turn down a joint for the first time in his life. There's a pattern-breaking discipline in him that's new, powerful, and exciting — because of Christ.*

*I experience joy when a perpetually angry guy (whom we all steer clear of if we don't want to be contaminated by his attitude) has a personality that's a pleasure to be around, with laughter accompanying his conversations.*

*I am surprised by joy when my friends speak the answers to the questions on my heart that we haven't shared with each other yet. Moments like that reinforce the truth that God is aware of my struggles. He's involved in my life at an intimate level, and I know I'm not forgotten or abandoned by him.*

*Joy, for me, is knowing as concretely as I know my name and my birthday that God is real and he loves me personally, and that I'm never alone and he can be trusted with my heart.*

*Mom, in spite of the agony I feel on my bad days, I'm grateful for what God is doing in my life. How I wish that pain of this magnitude didn't accompany my personal growth, especially the suffering of my victim's family and my own family. But I am reminded of something Tim Hansel wrote: "Joy is a process, a journey — often muffled, sometimes detoured; a mystery in which we participate, not a product we can grasp. It grows and regenerates as we have the courage to let go and trust the process. Growth and joy are inhibited when we say 'if only,' enhanced when we realize that failures and difficulties are not only a critical part of the process, but are our very opportunities to grow."*[23]

I'm discovering that any joy in the midst of this horrendous ordeal is a surprising gift from God. The only way I can recognize and embrace the gift when it comes is by recalling and practicing what Paul wrote to the Hebrews: "We do this by keeping our eyes on Jesus, the champion who initiates and perfects our faith. Because of the joy awaiting him, he endured the cross, disregarding its shame. Now he is seated in the place of honor beside God's throne."[24]

Mom, I desire for all of us healing and rest. I pray that your heart will smile.

## EXPLORING YOUR OWN GRACE PLACE

Most of us experience joy when we observe people we love celebrating good news or special occasions. It's easy to feel joyful when a baby is born or when people gather to honor someone at a birthday, graduation, or anniversary party. It's also natural to feel a relaxed, "all is right with the world" kind of happiness when we find a quiet place at a beach or in the mountains where we can breathe deeply and take in the splendor of God's creation. Sometimes we find joy in a special chair in our home where we curl up with a good book and relish the pleasure of some quiet time to ourselves. But we might not be as quick to recognize or appreciate the other "flavors" of joy — those that are harder won and sometimes enjoyed only after we've stood bereft at what appears to be an "empty tomb" in our life.

1. How do you define *joy*? What brings you happiness? Is there a special place, person, or occasion that always brings joy to your heart and refreshment to your soul?

2. Are joy and happiness the same thing for you? If there's a difference, what sets joy apart from happiness?

3. On a scale of 1 to 10 (with 10 being highest), how do you rate your sense of joy during this time in your life? Why?

| 1 | 2 | 3 | 4 | 5 | 6 | 7 | 8 | 9 | 10 |
|---|---|---|---|---|---|---|---|---|---|

I've lost my joy.　　My joy comes and goes,　　I am *delighting* in life!
but I'm OK.

4. Mary Magdalene had a unique life that included several surprising encounters during the time she knew Jesus. Which of the following experiences from her life do you identify with the most? Why?

 ✤ Jesus set her free from a past filled with anguish.

 ✤ Mary was part of Jesus' inner circle in which friends bonded and she got to know Jesus intimately.

144

✦ She had an empty-tomb moment when it appeared that Jesus was gone.

✦ She experienced the empty-tomb reality when she discovered that Jesus was alive and powerfully at work in her life.

5. Both Diana Pintar and Jason Kent have experienced situations that could have permanently stolen their joy, but they discovered great delight in unexpected places. What did you learn from their stories about cultivating joy?

6. Meditate on these Scriptures:

✦ "You have given me greater joy than those who have abundant harvests of grain and new wine." (Psalm 4:7 NLT)

✦ "Dear brothers and sisters, when troubles come your way, consider it an opportunity for great joy." (James 1:2 NLT)

✦ "Don't be dejected and sad, for the joy of the LORD is your strength!" (Nehemiah 8:10 NLT)

✦ "You have turned my mourning into joyful dancing. You have taken away my clothes of mourning and clothed me with joy." (Psalm 30:11 NLT)

Which of these verses describes what you have personally experienced about true joy? Or are you still trying to find your joy? That's OK. Being honest with God about your journey is the first step in making progress toward a level of intimacy with him that leads to joy.

CHAPTER 7

# A Different Kind
# of Liberty

Freedom is an inside job.
Sam Keen

My heart skipped a beat when I noticed the bold letters beneath the official seal for the State of Florida: "Office of Executive Clemency." The photocopied letter from the coordinator of that office was addressed to Jason's attorney. More than three years had passed since Jason had submitted an application for clemency. Finally an official response had arrived.

The letter informed Jason's attorney that the Florida Parole Commission, a group of three people who make all recommendations involving which cases will be heard before the Executive Clemency Board, had recommended that the board consider taking the most preliminary step in response to our son's application. This did not necessarily mean that the four-person board — which included the state's governor and attorney general — would give Jason a hearing regarding the possibility of commuting his life-without-the-possibility-of-parole sentence to a set number of years, but the letter was the first good news we had received in a very long time. The Florida Parole Commission had issued a favorable report to the executive clemency board, which meant the parole commission believed Jason's case merited consideration. My hopes were soaring!

A few days later, Jason's attorney arranged to meet with Gene and me, and during a lunch together we energetically made plans for our next steps. The attorney asked if we could make the five-hour drive to Tallahassee within the next few weeks so he could arrange for us to meet members of the parole commission, the attorney to the governor, and perhaps additional members of the executive clemency board. At these meetings we would have an opportunity to speak about our son regarding his record as an inmate, his achievements while incarcerated, and his plans and specific goals, should he ever be allowed to walk in freedom. It would be important for the clemency board to understand that our family could provide Jason with a place to live, income-producing work, and accountability if his sentence was commuted to a set number of years. Gene and I made careful notes throughout the two-hour meeting and returned home.

Forty-eight hours later, the phone rang at our home, and Gene picked up the receiver. Quickly walking to my office, he said, "Carol, it's important. Please pick up an extension."

I was surprised to hear the voice of Jason's attorney, calling so soon after our face-to-face meeting. He is always upbeat and has an energized, engaging personality, but after we exchanged the usual pleasantries, his voice became serious, even somber, as he said, "I have some disappointing news. I've received another letter from the coordinator of the Office of Executive Clemency, stating that what would have been the next step in the process has been denied. There won't even be a hearing."

I could hardly breathe. So many hopes and dreams were based on this process, and it was the only open door we had left that could have resulted in eventual freedom for our son. Tears were already spilling down my cheeks as Gene tried to keep the conversation going. Finally I tried to talk — but all I could do was state what we already knew, incredulity rising in my voice.

"But that first letter you received was dated only nine days before this second one. J.P.'s application, which has been making its way to the top of the parole commission's stack for *three years*, has already been denied, without a hearing? While we were meeting with you, just two days ago, the clemency board's office was posting a letter denying Jason the next step in this process? He's not asking for a Get-Out-of-Jail-Free card. He's asking the executive clemency board to evaluate his background, his crime, his record since he was first incarcerated ten years ago, and consider if keeping him locked up for the rest of his life, at a cost to taxpayers now estimated to be one million dollars per lifer, would best serve the State of Florida — or would it be conceivable that someday in the distant future he could be allowed to become a contributing member of society. We submitted over one hundred letters of support from people who know our son and have written on his behalf, along with petitions signed by thousands more people."

I took a breath in the middle of my tirade. I could feel fear mingled with my anger as I finally arrived at the questions that were gnawing at my gut. "Tell us, please, do you know of *anyone* in the history of your work on clemency cases who has my son's conviction — first-degree murder — who has had his sentence commuted to a set number of years? Or is that so politically unpopular that it won't even be considered?"

The attorney paused and said he'd have to do some more research in order to answer those questions. But I already knew the answers — at least from the recent past — because I'd checked the Internet for clemency cases in Florida during the past two terms of office for previous governors, and the trend has been toward lifetime punishment, not rehabilitation and restoration. Though we had longed for a miracle of mercy, I had wondered, when Gene and I were gathering the documentation for Jason to use in his application process, if we were simply trying to buy a few more years of hope for our son. What price does a parent put on that?

Now I realized, at a new rock-bottom level, that Jason would be in prison for the rest of his natural life. I created a mental picture of a worst-case-scenario. Even if he waited to apply for clemency again until he'd served twenty-five years, I convinced myself he would never walk in freedom. Or maybe he would be released when he became so elderly or so deathly ill that the government no longer wanted to pay for his health care.

Despair settled over me like a cloud. I put the phone down, and Gene finished the conversation with the attorney. I felt too sick to speak.

That night, I created a prison of my own making. I began to cry—not ladylike, sad tears, but body-shaking, nose-running, audibly wailing kind of sobbing from the depths of my aching heart. Gene put his arms around me, but I pushed him away. I didn't want my husband's touch, which in the past had always been comforting. I wanted to feel the depths of the pain because my only child would soon be experiencing it himself.

Once again I felt angry with God. *Why* had he allowed us to hope one more time, only to receive such a cold and insensitive response from the governor's attorney? Why couldn't we have at least been allowed to have the recommended opportunity for a hearing? Why hope? Why try? Why bother? God was not going to help us.

The next day was Saturday, and Gene told me he would drive to the prison early for visitation and break the news to Jason. I knew I couldn't handle seeing the disappointment on his face. I told Gene I'd be there by noon.

I drove the forty miles to the prison and parked in the large lot outside the razor wire. As I went through security, I had the routine pat-down. I heard the first heavy metal door close behind me as I picked up my visitation paperwork. The second door opened to the large room where many families had already gathered. When my eyes landed on J.P., my tears immediately started to brim over. We are allowed one embrace when we arrive and one embrace when we leave. My young son held me as I burst into sobs. No words were needed. He knew that I knew there would be no clemency hearing, and he would have to wait a mandatory five years to file the paperwork again, followed by the three to four years it usually takes for a request for a hearing to rise to the top of the pile, with the same uncertainty and political challenges we faced this time around. I sensed that he knew as well as I did that there would never be a commutation of his sentence to a set number of years that would eventually lead to freedom.

And yet, Jason did not appear to be upset. He wasn't angry and disheartened the way I was because of the "rubber stamp" rejection of his carefully prepared application for a clemency hearing. In fact, he seemed totally at peace — something I never thought possible. After we sat down together, he said, "Mom, we've done everything we can do. The petitions have been signed. The letters have been written. The application has been filed. We are at the end of our human ability to do anything else. The rest is up to God. And, Mom, if I am never released in this lifetime, remember that life is very short. In the blink of an eye, this life will be over, and we'll all be *truly* free. Eternity will have begun. And it won't be long."

That did it! The tears started rolling down my cheeks again. My incarcerated son was reminding me of one of the synonyms of the word *freedom*. It's *sovereignty*. God is sovereign, and he is totally in control of my future and Jason's future and my husband's future. He is in control, and I am not! Frankly, on my bad days, I don't like that one bit. On good days, however, I realize that our son's lack of freedom on the outside has resulted in a freedom on the inside that he might never have experienced to this degree if he had lived his entire life outside of the prison walls.

## The Surprise "Inside"

As an American, I have defined *freedom* as having the opportunity to go where I want to go, choose what I want to do, and make decisions without being bound by the rules of someone more powerful than I am. On the surface, it sounds like the complete antithesis of what my son experiences every day. I asked Jason to describe a typical day at the prison.

5:00 a.m. — I wake up and listen to a news program on the radio.

5:30 a.m. — My cell door opens and the lights come on.

6:00 a.m. — Inmates go to the chow hall for breakfast.

7:00 a.m. — All inmates are back in their cells and locked down for "count" and a shift change. (Inmates are counted by corrections officers several times a day.)

8:00 a.m. — The cell doors open and some inmates go to their jobs on the compound while others exercise in the yard.

11:00 a.m. — The recreation yard closes and inmates go back to their dormitories.

11:30 a.m. — We are locked in our cells and another count takes place.

12:00 p.m. — Cells open and we go to the chow hall for lunch.

1:30 p.m. — The yard opens for recreation again. Some inmates take classes in the chapel or in the education building.

3:30 p.m. — All inmates must return to their cells.

4:00 p.m. — We are locked in and another count takes place.

4:30 p.m. — Cells open and we go to the chow hall for dinner.

5:30 p.m. — The yard opens for recreation and sometimes chapel services take place.

7:00 p.m. — The yard closes.

7:45 p.m. — We are locked in our cells and another count takes place.

8:15 p.m. — The cell doors open and inmates can watch the television in the dayroom or stay in their cells.

10:00 p.m. — We are locked in our cells and another count takes place.

10:30 p.m. — The cell doors open and we can watch television in the dayroom or stay in our rooms.

11:00 p.m. — We are locked in for the night.

This agenda of my son's days is shockingly different from the variety represented in my day planner. It is filled with five mandated inmate inventory times and contains no freedom of choice. The rules must be followed, and variation is not open for discussion. As Jason reminds me, "It's prison, Mom. It's just the way it is."

So where is the "surprise" in this monotonous routine? It has everything to do with attitude. As I observed my son after he'd heard that he would not have a hearing on his application for clemency, I realized he not only understands what inner freedom is; he is also teaching his mother the secret to liberty of the heart.

A few days after he had held me, sobbing, in his arms, Jason sent me this letter.

*Dear Mom,*

*Yesterday I felt I was able to love, encourage, and bless you for once, where normally I've been the recipient of your love. It was a privilege for me to give back to you. God has been filling me with more of himself, and I am truly at peace. Out of his peace and love within, it's easy to pour it out on others, but it's a special treat to pour it out on you. I love you, and I'm grateful for how you've always been there for me and tried to comfort, protect, rescue, and help me throughout my life.*

*God is doing something powerful within me, and I'm very aware that I'm unworthy. Yet I find myself often speaking words that sustain the weary. I'm starting to experience something the prophet Isaiah wrote about: "The Master, GOD, has given me a well-taught tongue, so I know how to encourage tired people. He wakes me up in the morning, wakes me up, opens my ears to listen as one ready to take orders."[1] And I know he is speaking to me personally about my own life too. Everything I find myself saying to others is a "sermon" to myself as well. I am nothing more than a fellow student, pilgrim, and spiritual traveler.*

*One of the ways I'm experiencing more inner peace and spiritual freedom is through choosing to go to God in prayer early and often. First, before I try to strategize a plan or a path through the mazes of life, I ask him to make me wiser. Not because I have any innate ability to understand his plan, but because I am quicker than ever to turn to the only one who cares more than all of us and has the actual plan for our lives in hand. He desires conversation, fellowship, friendship, and communion. Sometimes I barely know what I'm talking about, and I live up to such a small amount of my potential — but I'm making progress.*

*I'm learning that it really is all about God and not about us. It's his-story (history), after all, and he allows us to play starring roles in his spectacular drama. The news Dad shared with me feels like a setback in the story of our lives. We're currently living through a crisis point, a transition in our journey where the tone of the "sound track" of our drama changes to one of tension and uncertainty. We know the story could turn in either direction. But our real struggle is a spiritual one. Will we turn toward truth, life, and transcendence, or will we curse the darkness and rage against a sense of futility, pounding our fists against the air with groans of frustration? We are already blessed in Christ. Romans 8:28[2] was true last week when you received the discouraging news, and it's still true today.*

*Life is short; time is a-wasting, and it's over for this stage of the play when God decides. Our Director is perfectly good and completely powerful, so we're safe even when this curtain closes. But remember, it's only the intermission — the best part of the story unfolds in the next scene.*

*I'm so glad God cast you and Dad in the role of my parents! I've never been very good at saying stuff like this, but you look beautiful, and Dad is fortunate to have you as his wife. I know this weekend was your fortieth wedding anniversary, and I'm sorry it was such a sad time for you. I love you so very much, Mom, and I pray that we, as a family, will continue to grow into a deeper and more transparent relationship with our Lord, Savior, King, and Friend, Jesus Christ.*

*With love and prayers,*

*J.P.*

Jason's words comforted me. My spirits began to lift, and I realized that God was answering my prayers for my son. J.P. continues to be drawn into an intimate love relationship with his heavenly Father, and his reflections echoed the truth the psalmist discovered: "I run in the path of your commands, for you have set my heart free."[3] I don't always want to admit it, but the most valuable kind of freedom we can experience in this lifetime is not physical — as much as I still want to see Jason physically freed from prison. The deepest freedom is spiritual, and laying hold of it is an inside job.

Of all the people whose stories are told in Scripture, perhaps none of them remind me of this truth better than Peter. Like my son, Peter had to face the horror and shame of personal failures he never dreamed would be part of his biography. Peter loved Jesus with passion and served him with boldness. And yet when the pressure was on in a way he had never experienced before, Peter stunned himself with how poorly he handled the situation. Fortunately, he discovered that his human limitations in following and honoring Jesus in no way limited Jesus' grace toward him. Peter's story reminds all of us that we can experience freedom on the inside, even when we blow it in our walk with God.

## The Peter Principle

I am surprised by Jesus' choice of disciples. They formed a rather motley crew, and Peter, called by Jesus from his career as a fisherman, was not always a team player. He was a dedicated but often arrogant disciple. He had a hot temper, was presumptuous, was both fearful and bold, passive and aggressive — and he betrayed the One to whom he vowed absolute devotion. Jesus knew Peter's defects, but he picked him anyway. And he forgave him for his multiple offenses.

I'm attracted to Peter's high energy and spontaneity. Imagine the fun of traveling with him during Jesus' public teaching ministry. He could be comically impulsive — twice jumping out of a boat fully clothed! He sometimes challenged Jesus, and he had a habit of speaking out of turn. But he also demonstrated fervent commitment and faith.

Peter's life could play out as a multiple-episode docudrama. Let's turn down the lights for a few minutes and review just a few captivating scenes at the end of Jesus' ministry.

**Scene 1.** The band of brothers who has spent three years walking, talking, and ministering with Jesus makes its way to the upper room to celebrate the traditional Passover meal together. Suddenly Jesus surprises the disciples with the most unlikely act. He gets up from the table, removes his robe, ties a towel around his waist, pours water into a basin, and begins to wash and dry the feet of each of his friends. When Jesus gets to Peter, the disciple protests, "No ... you will never ever wash my feet!"[4] Jesus replies, "Unless I wash you, you won't belong to me."[5] Peter enthusiastically responds, "Then wash my hands and head as well, Lord, not just my feet!"[6] Peter's wholehearted love for his Master is obvious. He wanted to be all Christian, all the time.

**Scene 2.** Later, during their meal, Jesus tells his disciples that he will be betrayed by Judas, but Peter and the others don't get what he's talking about. After Judas flees the room, Jesus indicates that the last chapter of his earthly life is about to unfold. Then he gives them a new commandment that is to supersede all others: "Love each other. Just as I have loved you, you should love each other. Your love for one another will prove to the world that you are my disciples."[7] Jesus tells them that where he is going next, they cannot follow until their own work on earth is done.

Peter doesn't understand, and he asks his dearest Friend why he can't come with him now, even saying, "I'm ready to die for you."[8] Now, I call that radical friendship! Which one of my friends would I die for right now? Jesus responds with a shocking statement: "Die for me? I tell you the truth, Peter — before the rooster crows tomorrow morning, you will deny three times that you even know me."[9]

It's hard for me to imagine what Peter thought and felt after hearing this. Was he stricken to his tender core, horrified by the idea that he could be capable of betraying the One he loved and served with all his heart and soul? Or did he think, *No way! I would never do what Jesus just described! I'll show him that he can trust me, no matter what the future holds.* After all, Peter was known for being cocky at times, and he had little comprehension yet of how his journey was about to change course.

**Scene 3.** After their last evening together, during which Jesus offers a great deal of prophetic teaching that his disciples barely understand, the small group of men leave the upper room and follow Jesus across a valley to the garden of Gethsemane. There, in a grove of olive trees, Jesus is betrayed by Judas and then arrested, tied up, and taken to the high priest's house. Peter and another disciple follow. The other disciple had connections that got him inside, but Peter is left behind in the courtyard. That brings us to the dreadful moment in the disciple's life story that Jesus foretold.

A servant girl approaches Peter in the courtyard and says, "You also were with Jesus of Galilee."[10]

> In front of everybody there, he denied it. "I don't know what you're talking about."
>
> As he moved over toward the gate, someone else said to the people there, "This man was with Jesus the Nazarene."
>
> Again he denied it, salting his denial with an oath: "I swear, I never laid eyes on the man."
>
> Shortly after that, some bystanders approached Peter. "You've got to be one of them. Your accent gives you away."
>
> Then he got really nervous and swore. "I don't know the man!"
>
> Just then a rooster crowed. Peter remembered what Jesus had said: "Before the rooster crows, you will deny me three times." He went out and cried and cried and cried.[11]

Peter's shame must have been intense considering the confidence Jesus had expressed in him at other times and the authority Jesus planned to give him: "And now I'm going to tell you who you are, *really* are," Matthew's gospel records Jesus as telling Peter early in their friendship. "You are Peter, a rock. This is the rock on which I will put together my church, a church so expansive with energy that not even the gates of hell will be able to keep it out."[12] Just imagine yourself in Peter's sandals in his overwhelming moment of comprehension and self-reproach. In a Roman courtyard, with his Friend tied up inside the house, he betrayed the One he loved — not just once, but *three times!* — just as Jesus had said he would.

As we turn the lights back up, let's consider the rest of Peter's story. Good news! His dreadful personal failure did not put an end to Peter's relationship with and usefulness to Jesus. In fact, Mark says that the angels guarding Jesus' tomb after the resurrection told Mary Magdalene to inform Peter *first* about the miracle of life after death. (I love to imagine *that* scene, when Peter got the report!) The very One he had sinned against so horrifically extended a merciful invitation to restoration, freeing Peter to leave his guilt and broken sense of self behind. From there, Peter went forward to become a "fisher of men" and a "rock" in the foundation of the church.

What a glorious surprise for this far-from-perfect man! Jesus understood the depth of Peter's love for him. He not only forgave Peter, but he also entrusted him with the monumental job of establishing the Christian church on earth. The rest of Peter's journey was an adventure, to say the least, and even though he died a gruesome martyr's death, his impact for Jesus was everlasting.

## Redemption Prevails

For those who love Christ, personal sin and failure need not spell "The End" of our story. Because of examples like Peter, I can hope and pray that Jason, while certainly not a martyr, will have a profound impact for Jesus, no matter his physical circumstances. He is experiencing a new kind of freedom inside prison walls. Rather than giving up on life because of his personal failures and the shocking way the course of his life changed as the result of his choices, he knows more than ever about the power of redemption that frees the spirit, calms the heart, and makes way for purposeful living in the most unexpected circumstances. Perhaps no freedom is more meaningful than that of being liberated from shame and guilt and set back on a path toward serving Christ.

As I speak at large and small gatherings throughout the U.S. and overseas, sharing the story of our journey with Jason, I discover (to my profound relief) that I am not alone in loving a lifer. And I am not the only one to have the course of my life abruptly and permanently changed as a result of a crime. Sometimes I need to be reminded of these facts, as sad as they are for everyone concerned.

In August 2008, I was one of several speakers at the Extraordinary Women Conference held in Griffin, Georgia, not far from Atlanta. It was always a privilege to participate in these events, and this high-energy weekend was no exception. My speaking assignment on this tour of several cities was to share our family's journey, based on my book *A New Kind of Normal*. My goal was to challenge each listener to make hope-filled choices when the life she once had or dreamed of turns out to be much more painful than she ever anticipated.

Two days after the conference ended, an e-mail arrived from a woman who had attended. Tammy Wilson has taught me much about the "other side" of a kind of forgiveness that liberates the heart and contributes to God's work of redemption in the midst of devastating circumstances. While being forgiven and granted the grace to let go of personal guilt is a freeing experience, the act of forgiving and letting go of resentment is every bit as profound in its power to transform the person who has been harmed. The story of a person who forgives from the heart contains a significant element of surprise in itself, simply because human beings, by nature, are not very forgiving. When we are deeply wounded, our natural and understandable reaction is to lash out at the person or situation that has harmed us — or to retreat, protect ourselves, and silently punish the offender by withholding grace. What we sometimes don't realize, however, is that by keeping the fire burning under our resentment and holding on to our hurt and anger, we actually increase our suffering and trap ourselves in a cycle of blame and sorrow that can make our lives a living hell.

Lewis Smedes wrote, "When you release the wrongdoer from the wrong,… you set a prisoner free, but you discover that the real prisoner was yourself."[13] Freedom on the inside is a two-way street. When the hearts of those on both sides of a painful or shattering event become liberated by forgiveness, grace pours in from a supernatural source. The result can be mental, emotional, and spiritual freedom that is surprising, humbling, and inspiring. Sometimes it's the only thing that finally makes life seem worth living again.

## Miracles *Do* Happen — Tammy's Story

*Carol,*

*I thoroughly enjoyed this weekend's Extraordinary Women Conference. I have to tell you my story so you will understand a little of why your testimony about your situation was a message I needed to hear.*

*On December 9, 1995, my mom, Tonya Sargeant, was shot and killed by a young man named Matthew Ben Rodriguez. When the shooting occurred, Matthew and two friends were planning to rob the Eckerd's store in St. Petersburg where my mom was the assistant manager. The three guys were later arrested, and two of them are now serving life sentences without the possibility of parole.*

*My mom was a daughter, sister, and friend to many before becoming a wife, then a mother. I was honored to be her daughter. She was the most compassionate, kind, loving person anyone could ever meet. Mom made everyone around her feel special.*

*Before her death, Mom and her third husband, Virgil, with whom she was extremely happy, had recently come to visit us for Thanksgiving. While here in Georgia, Mom spent a lot of time telling us family stories, what life was like for her as a child, and many other things she had never told us before. When it was time for her to return to Florida, she said something that I thought sounded so strange: "If something ever happens to me, don't hate the person, only what they did." Talk about bizarre! As she closed the car door and she and Virgil pulled away, I looked at my husband and said, "What in the world is wrong with my mom?"*

*Almost two weeks later, on December 8, Mom called me at work. She wanted to talk, but I was really busy, so I told her I would call her later. After we hung up, I did not remember our conversation until it was too late to call back. I had no idea, of course, that I would never get to talk to her again.*

*December 9 had been a regular Saturday for me. I don't remember anything special about that day until "the call." At approximately 1:30 a.m. on Sunday morning, December 10, the phone rang. It was my stepfather, Curt, and I knew it was not good news. I remember Curt's exact words: "Missy [my cousin] called and said that your mom has been shot and killed." I immediately got mad because I knew someone was playing a really terrible joke on us. I told Mom's second husband that I would find out who was saying such ridiculous stuff and call him back.*

*I called Mom's home number to see if I could track her and Virgil down, but no one answered the phone. I called my grandmother and aunt, who both live in Florida. No answer. As a last resort, I called the hospital in St. Petersburg and talked to a nurse in the emergency room, who confirmed my worst fears — that my beautiful mother had been shot and killed. The nurse was very gracious and probably broke a privacy law or two by telling me the truth. I'm sure she heard the panic in my voice and knew that I needed to know two things: first, that Mom was gone, and second, that she did not suffer — she had died instantly. As I dropped the phone and almost collapsed, my sweet husband took the receiver and thanked the compassionate nurse.*

*Things are a blur from there; however, I can say that until that point in my twenty-five years of life I had never faced anything so tragic. My twenty-three-year-old sister, Kim, was out of town, and we didn't know how to reach her. Her father-in-law managed to track her down and tell her the horrible news. She then had to ride four hours in a car from Alabama to Georgia so we could fly to Florida the next morning to deal with Mom's death. My brother, Patrick, was only eighteen at the time. He and Kim and I went to the airport together to board the plane. I remember thinking as I backed the car out of my driveway, my life is totally over! I was sure I would not survive the next few days, much less the rest of my life, without my mom around to call for support and unconditional love. She was not supposed to die at the age of forty-four.*

*The longest three days of my life were during the time when we had no idea who had shot our mom, or why. It was hard to even go to the grocery store without wondering if the person in line beside us was the one who had ended the life of a very special angel.*

*After the police caught the young men involved, we went through trials for two of them and many sleepless nights before verdicts were reached that we felt were appropriate. Some of our relatives and friends wanted the offenders to get the death penalty, but our immediate family did not feel that Mom would have wanted that. Fortunately, the assistant district attorney at the time didn't think a jury would give the men the death penalty anyway, so that punishment wasn't one of the jurors' options.*

*Looking back, I know that God sustained us through those terrible days and in some ways prepared us. We knew that Mom was in a better place. She was a believer and lived her life every day for the Lord. Her daily devotional book, bookmarked on the day of her death, was a reflection on Matthew 6:19–20: "Lay not up for yourselves treasures upon earth, where moth and rust doth corrupt, and where thieves break through and steal: But lay up for yourselves treasures in heaven, where neither moth nor rust doth corrupt, and where thieves do not break through nor steal." Mom truly laid up her treasures in heaven; she would have given the shirt off her back to anyone in need. She was a lady after God's own heart, and I firmly believe that she wanted us to forgive the young men involved in her murder.*

*Nevertheless, that Christmas 1995 was absolutely horrible. No*

*one in our family put up a Christmas tree. We were angry and
miserable. Mother's Day 1996 was the same, filled with lots of hurt
and pain associated with a holiday that had meant so much to
us prior to Mom's death. When my sister found out shortly after
Mom died that she was pregnant, our feelings were bittersweet. The
one thing Mom desired more than anything in this world was to
have a grandchild. On September 26, 1996, Mom's first grandchild
was born, and though it was one of the best events in my family's
history, it was also very sad to know that Mom would not be a part
of the celebration of this little life. Since that time, Mom became a
grandmother to three other beautiful children, who one fine day in
heaven will finally get to meet her.*

*It's hard to believe that thirteen years have gone by since she was killed.
Her presence is still missed at every holiday gathering, and many times
we just don't talk about her, for fear of causing others pain.*

*About a year after Mom died, I felt God tugging at my heart to
forgive those who took her from me. I have to be honest: I did
not want to do it. But I wrote a letter to the man who pulled the
trigger — Matthew Ben Rodriguez — telling him that I forgave him. I
never mailed the letter.*

*The reason I am writing to you now, Carol, is because, as I heard
you speak, I was so struck by your compassion — not only for families
whose children have committed crimes, but also for those who
have lost loved ones as a result of those crimes. I know I was at that
conference not to hear what the other speakers said (although they
were good), but to be inspired by your message of freedom through
forgiveness. I have forgiven Matt Rodriguez for his actions, though I
must say it has been a struggle.*

*After I got home from the conference, I looked up your son, Jason,
online, and according to the Department of Corrections, he is
at Hardee Correctional Institution in Bowling Green, Florida. If
he is still there, it is the same facility in which Matt Rodriguez is
incarcerated. My prayer has long been that someone at the Hardee
prison would be able to share the love of Christ with Matt. I think*

*my mom somehow had a premonition about the future because of that "strange" thing she said to us prior to her murder: "If anything ever happens to me, don't hate the person, only what they did." Those words have stuck with me all these years.*

*Please know that as I pray for Matt Rodriguez and the other two men involved, I will now pray for Jason and you as well. Thank you for allowing God to use your tragedy to impact others. May God continue to bless you and your family.*

*Tammy Wilson*

## Free Indeed

There are times in life when I sense that God is at work in ways that can only be explained in the supernatural dimension. Reading Tammy's letter filled my heart with hope, and I had a sense that there would be more to this story. I had a strong desire to participate in whatever God was doing in this situation. I began to pray for wisdom and discernment.

Gene and I are not allowed to initiate phone calls to our son, so I printed Tammy's e-mail and mailed it to Jason. What happened next still makes me weep. At visitation the next week, my son told me that when he read Tammy's letter, he immediately knew who she was asking about. I could hardly believe my ears when he said, "Mom, Matthew Rodriguez is one of my best friends here at Hardee."

Jason went on to tell me about what happened after he received Tammy's letter. He approached his friend and asked, "Matt, is your middle name Ben?" Matt replied, "Yes, it is." Jason said, "Then I have a letter for you." Jason handed Matt Tammy's letter, and as Matt read her words, he began to weep. Jason told me that Matt is now a vibrant Christian who is growing in his faith. He also told me that Matt's sister comes to visit him and that he would probably be in the visitation room with her that day.

About an hour later, Jason indicated to me that Matt's sister had arrived and Matt would be coming out to meet with her. When Matt arrived in the visitation area and saw Jason and me across the room, he came over to our table and knelt down next to me with tears in his eyes. He told me that he had written Tammy a letter but didn't know how to reach her. He said, "God has done so much in my life, and I want to be able to ask for forgiveness from the family and to tell them how sorry I am for the sorrow my actions have caused. Mrs. Kent, will you ask Tammy Wilson if there is an address where I can send my letter so she will receive it?" By this time, Jason had tears in his own eyes, and I could hardly control my emotions.

When I got home from the prison that day, I wrote an e-mail to Tammy, sharing the series of events and my tremendous surprise in finding out that Matthew not only resided at Hardee but was a close friend of my son's. I added:

> *I know it isn't an accident that Matt is in the same prison as Jason and that you wrote to me following the women's conference in Georgia. I want you to know that Matt is considerate and well mannered, is a tremendous encouragement and support to our son, and has a vibrant faith. Matt told me he has been incarcerated since he was twenty years old, and he's thirty-three now. From our brief meeting, I can tell he is deeply repentant. He wants to make contact with you, if you are open to that possibility. If you are willing to receive a letter from him but would like your address to be anonymous to him, I can ask him to send the letter to me for safe delivery to you. Or if you feel comfortable having me give him your address, I would be happy to do so.*
>
> *Just know that this young man is not the man he once was and that he is fully aware of the deep pain and sorrow he has caused in your life. He wants to ask you and your family for forgiveness. Also, if it is ever in your heart to want to meet Matt, I'm sure he would be open to that—and he would probably be filled with so much emotion that he might have trouble speaking. For now, let me know if you are open to receiving his letter.*
>
> *What a privilege it is for me to pray for both you and for Matt.*

*I ache to think of the pain you have endured. Please know that I understand if you need to wait a while to respond to this note.*

I'm convinced that God had already been at work in Tammy's heart because she responded that very evening.

*Dear Carol,*

*I am thrilled beyond words to hear that Jason and Matt know each other. It has been my prayer for years that Matt would find peace. If Matt would like to send me a letter, that is fine. I am a little nervous just because of the situation, but I think this is a "God thing," and who am I not to do what I feel he is leading me to do?*

*Thank you for letting me know that Matt is a Christian and is growing in his relationship with God. I am so thankful that you shared my e-mail with your son and that he shared it with Matt, as I am not sure when I would have mailed him a letter — if ever. I have written letters to him numerous times but have never sent them. God is at work even now, and though I am anxious, I know he is working all this out for his glory. I pray that this will be an opportunity to grow and heal just a little more.*

*Tammy*

Tammy's graciousness and enthusiasm spoke volumes about a woman who has experienced the freedom on the inside that forgiveness produces. She demonstrates what Catherine Ponder describes so well: "When you hold resentment toward another, you are bound to that person or condition by an emotional link that is stronger than steel. Forgiveness is the only way to dissolve that link and get free."[14]

This story is big and miraculous, and it is still unfolding. You'll hear more in the next chapter. Jason and his victim's family may or may not ever have the opportunity for the same deep healing Matthew and Tammy are experiencing, but Jason can draw hope and comfort from stories like this one, stories that demonstrate for him "in the flesh" the forgiveness, redemption, reconciliation, and freedom from guilt and pain that is available through a relationship with Christ. And that's the kind of *inner* freedom that sets people free indeed.

166

## EXPLORING YOUR OWN GRACE PLACE

Freedom is something most of us take for granted. We make decisions about what our daily activities will be, and we move around at will. Freedom on the inside involves the ability to be at peace in the middle of circumstances that, humanly speaking, have the potential to make us feel confined or without a sense of control over the outcome of our lives. That kind of freedom can be hard-won, but along the way to attaining it we are often given opportunities to experience divine surprises and unexpected benefits.

1. What does the title of this chapter, "Liberty of the Heart," mean to you? In 2 Corinthians 3:17 (NASB), Paul writes, "Now the Lord is the Spirit, and where the Spirit of the Lord is, there is liberty." How is it possible to live in the middle of unresolved issues and tight spots and still experience inner freedom? In what ways have you experienced this kind of freedom in your life?

2. When you have been wronged by someone, what is your typical response?

    ❖ I am a "hot reactor." I get my emotions out on the table and no one has to guess what I'm feeling.

    ❖ I am a "slow boiler." I hide my feelings inside and say, "No problem," pretending everything is OK. But there's a bubbling cauldron of emotion welling up, and it eventually explodes.

    ❖ I stuff and deny my emotions, not wanting anyone to guess I'm upset or feel angry and resentful. I rarely let anyone see my feelings.

3. Peter is an intriguing Bible character in the New Testament. Which of the following details from his life do you most identify with? Why?

    ❖ He was energetic and spontaneous — sometimes speaking or acting impulsively without thinking about the consequences.

+ He said he loved Jesus enough to die for him, but he denied him three times — treating one of his best friends without loyalty or respect. When his faith was put to the test, he failed miserably.

+ Jesus understood how much Peter loved him, and in spite of the disciple's failures, Jesus extended extravagant forgiveness. Peter was also given the opportunity to do great ministry (which, in his case, was to establish the Christian church).

4. In this chapter, Jason Kent describes freedom on the inside in spite of living in a maximum security prison. What can you use from the lessons he's learned that might help you experience that kind of inner peace — even in the face of deep disappointments or having no tangible reason to hope for positive change?

5. Tammy Wilson has gone through an experience most of us will not face in this lifetime — the violent loss of her mother — that forever changed the rest of her life. She has been honest about her loss, pain, and anxiety, but she has kept the door of her heart open to God's healing and redemption through the liberation that comes through forgiveness and reconciliation. What have you learned from Tammy's story, and how can you apply it in your life today?

6. Write out your own definition of forgiveness. Then fill in these blanks and turn your words into a prayer: Lord, I need to forgive _____. My emotions of [anger, fear, resentment, etc.] _____ have kept me in a prison of my own making. I confess to you all wrongdoing and wrong thinking on my part, and I ask for your wisdom about what steps to take next that will move me in the direction of restoration, redemption, and true liberty of the heart. Amen.

CHAPTER 8

# DWELLING IN THE GRACE PLACE

## SURPRISED BY ADVENTURE

> The only way to live in this adventure—
> with all its danger and unpredictability
> and immensely high stakes—
> is in an ongoing, intimate relationship with God.
> **John Eldredge**

We were making big plans! I had been asked to speak at a conference center on Big Bear Lake in California on the first weekend in April. It was 1989, and Jason was thirteen years old. He would be heading into high school in the fall, and Gene thought a trip to Yosemite National Park would be the ideal way to spend some quality family time during Jason's spring break.

"Honey, check this out," Gene said enthusiastically. He had already marked the road atlas with a highlighter to show me our route from the Ontario (California) airport, and he spread the map, along with some brochures of rustic lodging options, in front of me. He hardly took a breath before continuing. "My favorite vacation when I was a kid was the year my parents took us on a train trip out west to visit relatives in Montana. I'll never forget seeing mountains for the first time and

169

fishing in a rushing stream, catching another trout every time I dipped my line into the water. I looked up and saw the biggest sky I'd ever laid eyes on. I want us to make more of these kinds of special memories with J.P. What do you think?"

Gene knew I was more of a hotel kind of girl, so I pretended to resist the thought of roughing it. But secretly I was pleased. I knew Gene was trying to create a once-in-a-lifetime experience for our family, and I loved watching his characteristically energetic approach to the planning.

Still thinking he had to convince me to participate, Gene went into his "salesman" mode. "Carol, they have cabins in the national park that we can rent, and in some areas they have indoor plumbing. It will be our back-to-nature experience of a lifetime. I know we'll all love it!"

His presentation had all the necessary ingredients: the promise of quality family time, wonders of nature we'd never seen before, exercise and fresh air, the thrill of new vistas, and the challenge of calculated risk. How could I say no to such an opportunity? I'm sure my speedy response surprised him. Looking up from the atlas, I said, "Let's do it — yes, let's go!" I'd be the photographer and record my guys as they took appropriate risks and hiked on rough terrain. I knew we would look back at the photographs and relive our adventure many times over.

As the date got closer, Gene made sure we had more information to whet our appetites for the trip. "Did you know that Yosemite National Park was one of the first wilderness parks in the United States? It has lots of waterfalls, and it covers nearly twelve hundred square miles. You know those pictures we've seen of the giant redwoods? We're going to see them in person! This park has waterfalls, mountains, valleys, wildlife, and a huge wilderness area."

Jason eagerly started a pile of the gear he was going to need for this special adventure. Through the years he had become an expert traveler and loved all parts of experiencing new places and exploring unknown territory. I was sure my enjoyment of my son's and husband's enthusiastic anticipation was as much fun as the journey itself would be.

Recently, I found a folder that contained Gene's notes on the Yosemite trip. It is hard to believe that this adventure had taken place two decades before. It seems like yesterday. Gene wrote down the details of a particularly memorable portion of our journey.

The drive to Yosemite was spectacular. When we arrived at our camp, we pulled up to our designated cabin. Carol was still getting things out of the car when Jason and I opened the door to our home away from home. The cabin was indeed rustic, besides being old, stinky, and dirty. A few multiple-legged bugs were on the counter in the kitchen. My son looked at me quizzically and asked, "Dad, are we really going to stay here? Mom will hate it!" But Carol proved to be a good sport, and we stayed. After all, we had already paid for the lodging!

The next morning I described to Carol and J.P. a terrific trail I had read about that led to the top of Lower Yosemite Falls. It was only about two miles long and supposedly well suited for novice hikers. They were game. After enjoying a huge pancake breakfast, we got ready for the "short" hike, donning shorts, caps, sunglasses, and athletic shoes. I threw some snacks, water, a few Band Aids, sunscreen, and insect repellant into a small backpack, and off we went to the trailhead.

The path was beautiful and easy to follow, and the first mile or so was on level ground. We soon found out, however, that the second leg would be uphill. No problem, though, because we were in good condition, and we were having fun. Jason was constantly venturing off in search of a less-traveled path or a spectacular view. Every so often we'd hear him yelling, "Hey, Mom and Dad, come look at this. Wow, I can't believe how cool this is!"

When we made the summit, we were delighted that we could see for miles. We could feel the spray from the Lower Falls and hear the distant roar of the Upper Falls. "It's only two more miles to the very top of the Upper Falls," I said. "Can we do it? How are you two feeling?" With unanimous enthusiasm, we took off toward our new goal.

The next two miles of switchbacks made the trail much steeper and more grueling. It was getting hot, and we were all sweating profusely with the exertion. But we trekked on. This was the adventure we were looking for!

After about three more hours, when we were really getting tired, the rush of water we had heard from a distance had amplified to a nearly deafening roar. Suddenly we were standing at the top of Upper Yosemite Falls!

Walking over to the edge of the falls was not forbidden, and the area was not fenced off. In fact, there were even handholds made of pipe embedded in the rock so hikers could hold on, lean over the side, and look toward the bottom. J.P. and I did — very cautiously! Carol couldn't even stand to watch us. But what a view J.P. and I had! We were over three thousand feet above the valley, with rock cliffs surrounding us, a perfect blue sky above us, and water rushing below us. God's glory was on magnificent display.

We found a spot to relax on the shore of the pool that formed near the edge of the falls just before it plunged over the cliff. Carol noticed a small sign posted by the pool which read,

IF YOU SWIM IN THESE WATERS, YOU WILL DIE!

We laughed at the bluntness of the statement, but the sobering truth of the message was obvious. Carol said, "I suppose that's a more effective sign than Swim at Your Own Risk or No Lifeguard on Duty." We all agreed that the unusual warning accomplished its purpose.

By now it was midafternoon, and we still had to hike all the way back the way we came, but at least it would be downhill. Easy, huh? We quickly discovered that scuttling downhill was nearly as tiring as hiking uphill. After nearly five more hours of grunting, panting, and wiping sweat off our grimy faces, we finally arrived back at the trailhead. J.P. was the first to speak. "Dad, can we do this again tomorrow?"

You've probably guessed the answer to that question! Our mission was accomplished. We'd had a never-to-be-forgotten family adventure that included risk, fun, novelty, hard work, satisfaction, and exhilaration. And in the retelling of our experience in the years since then, we have relived it many times over in our memories.

## Adventure's Challenge

I always thought I loved adventure, but when I married Gene Kent and became the mother of Jason, I began to understand a much deeper meaning of the word. An adventure can include uncertain experiences, even risk; it can feel frightening, even dangerous. But the upside of adventure is that it provides excitement, fulfillment, greater knowledge, and a sense of accomplishment. You may not like all aspects of the preparation, and there may be surprising obstacles in your path, but the goal is worthy of the sacrifice and the end result is a new kind of confidence, conviction, and courage to stay engaged with life, wherever it leads.

From the time Jason was young, he loved the intrigue associated with adventure, as well as the mental commitment required to soar beyond challenges he had faced before. In high school he was quick to encourage friends on his cross-country team to stay mentally focused when they were running, assuring them that they could make it across the finish line. It seemed natural when he chose to pursue a military career, and in 1993 when he received one of the approximately one thousand coveted appointments to the U.S. Naval Academy, Gene and I were thrilled for him. Staying the course throughout his years at Annapolis was filled with everything adventure requires: discipline, commitment to difficult tasks, the risk of danger or failure, the exhilaration of achievement, and the reward of completing a mission.

When Jason married just one year after graduation, he became a husband and a stepfather on the same day. He had big goals and knew that he and his wife and girls would experience adventures all over the world as a military family. He expected both his marriage and his military career to involve a combination of uncertainty (*How can I be a father and a protector to my stepdaughters?*), risk (*I could be sent on a military mission anywhere in the world and be separated from my family for long periods)*, and potential danger *(As a military officer I am prepared to give my life for my country)*. However, every time I talked to my son I recognized that, no matter what happened, he was willing to forge ahead because of the promise of fulfillment, personal growth, and purposeful impact.

Now, more than a quarter of my son's life has been lived behind bars. One of the biggest surprises to both him and to us as parents is that none of his higher education, leadership skills, or spiritual development have been wasted. Even though he is incarcerated, he has not been barred from being of service to others. God has continued to provide opportunities for him to experience adventure as he uses his gifts, training, and skills to positively impact those around him. He's currently taking his fifth group of inmates through Dave Ramsey's Financial Peace University course.[1] In each class, thirty-five to fifty men learn basic financial skills, including how to put together a workable budget — many of them for the first time in their lives. Jason has also helped facilitate a DVD teaching course called "Caring for People God's Way,"[2] leading two groups of inmates through follow-up discussions on dealing with emotions, relationships, and personal difficulties from a biblical perspective. Another part of his personal adventure behind bars is meeting with a racially diverse prayer group of twelve inmates who hold each other accountable for living out their faith through their language (no swearing), their actions (no inappropriate physical retaliation when they're angry), and their relationships (not hanging out with inmates who are going to drag them down spiritually or mentally). They get together weekly and pray for unity on the compound and for spiritual revival. In ways that bring a continual joyful surprise to my heart, my son is living out the ultimate adventure — a purposeful, intentional, sometimes risky and uncertain journey in the middle of uncharted territory.

What encourages me most about my son's journey now, however, is not related so much to what he *does or doesn't do* as to *who he is* and how he chooses to see his situation and the world. He has admitted to me that there are days when he "feels like crap" and like a failure in his personal impact on the lives of others. He told me, "Mom, sometimes people write to me as though I'm living for God the way the apostle Paul did! They think I'm doing a gigantic work for God in this prison. But there are days when I do nothing but survive. And there are other days when I do just one thing to make a difference in people's lives. Sometimes I have to *force* myself to live the life I know I'm called to live for God's glory. There are days I succeed and days I fail."

I get that, because that's my story too. Sometimes I take hold of the adventure offered in a new day and feel grateful that I can live for God's higher purposes; other times I crawl into a dark emotional hole because it seems like nothing changes and there's no point to any of it. The challenge for me and for Gene is to stay open to the surprise of adventure on our journey and to say yes to God. This letter from Jason encourages us to do just that.

*Dear Mom and Dad,*

*I was thinking the other day about that time, after I was beaten up in the county jail, when you arranged for me to have my front teeth repaired by an outside dentist. (Remember how different I looked after I successfully blocked most of the kicks with my mouth? Not a pretty sight.) Months after my two front teeth were broken off, I was transported from the jail to the dentist's office. I had not set foot outside the confines of the jail for a very long time, so to ride for even a short distance in a van and then sit in a dental chair in front of a huge window was actually peaceful. Two armed guards stood on either side of the window, but from my seat I could see the tree-shaded parking lot. I hadn't been enjoying the beauty of nature while being held in the county jail, of course, and the grounds of our state prisons are particularly stark. I think there is a total of about ten trees on the grounds of all fifty prisons in Florida!*

*Later I saw two other inmates who were in transit too, and I'll never forget how they looked. They were probably in their early sixties, but they both looked closer to ninety. They looked both sick and tired. I didn't know what their stories were, but I remember thinking how I didn't want to become like them someday.*

*Now, after these years behind bars with other lifers, I understand how a young man could become very old very fast. Imagine a lifetime of THIS. All your friends gone, all your dreams dead, all your energy spent. I see the hopelessness in men's eyes and the way they carry themselves. But I don't want to become like that! In fact, it almost makes me scream out loud—Seize the day! It's all we have. Live it as your last. Love like there's no tomorrow.*

*In prison, every day can easily bleed into the next. It's a lot like the movie Groundhog Day at times. There are not many things to separate each day from another like there are on the outside. It's easy to fall into the habit of procrastination because you can put things off. After all, there's an infinite number of the same kind of tomorrows ahead of you. The monotony can drag you down like a long, slow slog through quicksand. The challenge here is to find productive, positive ways to engage yourself.*

*I'm always reminding myself to seize the day—to make the most of the moments I have. We only have NOW to love and serve and show grace and mercy and to be good stewards of what we've been entrusted with. All of us, even prisoners, have some things we can offer—even if that's just our smile, our friendship, our encouragement, or our blessing. We can't wait to act, but we must love with Jesus as our guide TODAY. We might not have tomorrow.*

*I'm not saying that it's not tough to stay positive—especially in this atmosphere of laziness, lethargy, hopelessness, boredom, and lack of motivation. I must fight it every day. The peer pressure here is in the direction of quitting—dropping goals, dreams, hopes, vision, and mission. It's hard not to give into it when there is a tunnel in front of you for as far as the eye can see. But I must stand on God's statements in the Bible of what reality is because my current experience is not lining up. I must force myself to realize that God defines reality; my experience does not define him. Only with him as a guide will I make it. Left to myself I'll either fight continually (both mentally and spiritually), or I'll try to retreat or I'll die. I choose to stay engaged and to try to recognize the ways my life can still be an adventure, even within the walls and the monotony of prison.*

*Slowly I am learning that Jesus is my closest friend and the only one who truly understands what I'm going through. The fact that being incarcerated is my own fault doesn't lessen the pain of being here. That's why the more I can focus on eternity and the adventure of serving Christ today, the less I'm preoccupied with loneliness or any other problem as the result of my lost freedom. The truth is, somebody can be blessed by me today. I need to find that somebody and give what I can—a word, a Honey Bun, a soda, a smile, a handshake, a hug, a prayer. Hope is contagious, you know ...*

When your ongoing adventure includes an intimate relationship with God, there's a momentum on the journey that moves you forward with purpose and hope, no matter how rocky the path. And that kind of attitude and approach *is* contagious. Other people see what you're doing, and they join the quest for something more, something better, something worthy of their time and energy, because they know it's what Jesus would do if he walked their path today.

I find it helpful to look at examples of other people who've encountered challenging life experiences and have learned, sometimes through pain, wrong choices, and difficult roadblocks, how to embrace their physical, mental, and spiritual adventure once again. You've no doubt heard about a man named David who did just that.

## David's Surprising Legacy

If David lived at this time in history and his biographical summary was posted on the Internet by a speakers' bureau, it would create great interest and international demand. His résumé is filled with surprises.

Think of what it would be like to hear from a man who grew up as a sheepherder, then came into greater visibility as an unlikely giant killer, became a poet and a sought-after musician, and eventually became a king. I'd like to interview that person. If David appeared on *20/20* or *Dateline NBC*, perhaps we'd get some answers to these questions:

- How did you come from such humble beginnings and wind up as royalty?
- Did you have to fight getting a big head after you killed that giant when you were just a kid?
- Is writing poetry hard for you, or is it a natural gift?
- Which do you enjoy most? Playing music or leading people in your role as a king?
- Did you have greater adventures before or after you became famous?

However, the interview couldn't end there, because there's more to David's biography than the electrifying beginning. A skilled journalist would uncover the darker side of David's past, which included his roles as a betrayer, a liar, an adulterer, and a murderer. Perhaps the interviewer's questions would take a sharp turn after the first or second commercial:

- When did you first notice Bathsheba?
- How did you arrange to meet her?
- Where were you at the time her husband, Uriah, was killed in the front lines of duty?
- Did you have anything to do with the change in Uriah's military orders that led to his death?
- Would it be accurate to say you abused your power?
- Do you admit that you are a murderer?
- Did you make any mistakes as a father?
- If you could live your life over again, what would you do differently?[3]

The recorded biblical story of David's life does not gloss over his multiple failures. However, he will forever be remembered by God's surprising assessment of his heart: "God removed Saul and replaced him with David, a man about whom God said, 'I have found David son of Jesse, a man after my own heart. He will do everything I want him to do.'"[4]

David's whole life was an adventure. He lived with great conviction and gusto, but he also sinned repeatedly. He was quick to confess his sins, however, and he demonstrated genuine repentance. Here is just one example of the heart attitude that God loved in this flawed man.

> Have mercy on me, O God,
> > because of your unfailing love.
> Because of your great compassion,
> > blot out the stain of my sins.
> Wash me clean from my guilt.
> > Purify me from my sin.
> For I recognize my rebellion;
> > it haunts me day and night.
> Against you, and you alone, have I sinned;
> > I have done what is evil in your sight.
> You will be proved right in what you say,
> > and your judgment against me is just.
> For I was born a sinner —
> > yes, from the moment my mother conceived me.
> But you desire honesty from the womb,
> > teaching me wisdom even there.
>
> Purify me from my sins, and I will be clean;
> > wash me, and I will be whiter than snow.
> Oh, give me back my joy again;
> > you have broken me —
> > now let me rejoice.
> Don't keep looking at my sins.
> > Remove the stain of my guilt.
> Create in me a clean heart, O God.
> > Renew a loyal spirit within me.[5]

I love the fact that God did not withhold his blessing from David. Had the confession come to me, I might have been tempted to say, *You blew it big-time, David! You made your bed. Now you can just lie in it until you die. I gave you multiple opportunities to succeed. You could have accomplished so much if you hadn't given in to lust, deceit, and murder. I forgive you, but I won't bless you. You chose your own path, buddy. You will never have my approval again.*

But God had already ordained that David's many gifts would be used to make a profound difference in his generation, even though he had a heinous crime on his résumé. David was between a rock and a hard place many times. His life was filled with tabloid-worthy escapades that would have made front-page headlines in today's world. (I can identify because of the headlines our story got when my son was arrested.) David sinned greatly, but he learned his lessons. Although there were consequences for his actions, I believe the beginning of the new adventure of his life began after David prayed, "God, make a fresh start in me, shape a Genesis week from the chaos of my life."[6]

## So Where Is the Adventure Now?

Even if your journey isn't as dramatic as David's or as publicly embarrassing and heart-wrenching as our family's, there are no doubt times when you get stuck and need to be reminded that, no matter what you encounter on your road, there is hope for the future because of God's great compassion and grace. I find myself in constant need of this kind of encouragement.

Since Jason's incarceration I have had to learn how to contemplate the future very differently than I used to. And I've had to change my definition of *adventure*. Now it has far less to do with activities and feats that involve "living on the edge" and "pushing the limits" in the traditional sense. Instead, it usually involves seeing a need and finding a creative way of motivating people to lend a hand and make a difference in each other's lives. Gene and I feel called now to be advocates for those who cannot speak up for themselves. This includes encouraging individuals, churches, and organizations to get involved in the nonprofit organization we launched to benefit inmates and their families (visit www.SpeakUpforHope.org). Our mission frequently involves supporting other people as they risk doing something they've never done before. Our influence is sometimes direct; other times it's indirect, and we don't even know about it. When we do get to find out what others are doing as a result of our sharing our own adventure, we are often graced with surprises that make our challenges feel a little less burdensome.

Connecting Tammy Wilson and Matthew Rodriguez has been the most surprising and thrilling leg of that adventure so far. To help bring people like them together is an exciting undertaking that brings a great sense of fulfillment, mostly because of our growing understanding that the essence of spiritual adventure is saying yes to God. That's what Tammy and Matt are doing, and their adventure — both individually and together — continues to amaze and encourage me.

Less than two months after I received Tammy Wilson's note following the Extraordinary Women event at which she heard me speak about our family's "new kind of normal" since Jason's arrest and incarceration, a whole new chapter in Tammy's life was being written. After Tammy agreed to receive a letter from the man who had shot and killed her beloved mother, Matthew wrote to her immediately, and she wrote right back. Shortly after receiving her reply, Matthew sent me a letter that filled me in on some of the details surrounding his crime, his experience as a lifer like my son, and his humbled astonishment at the ways God is pouring out grace and redemption on him and on those he has harmed.

## A Future and a Hope — Matthew's Story

*Dear Mrs. Kent,*

*Thank you for your involvement in uniting me and Tammy Wilson. You are literally an answer to my prayers. It never ceases to amaze me how God reveals to us his divine plan and how far back in each of our lives he has been putting together the necessary pieces to facilitate his ultimate ends. I don't believe in coincidences. It is plain to see how tragedy in your life has given you a powerful testimony and a unique empathy for others. I can only pray that God will see fit to use my experiences in some way to help others who are seeking answers and meaning in the midst of their own heartaches.*

*I asked Jesus into my life when I was nine years old, but for most of my life I didn't have the relationship with God that I have now. My parents divorced when I was three years old, and my older sister, Erika, and I were raised by my mother. We had a lot of interaction with my mom's side of the family, which was big on love but short on God. My father, who was in the Navy, was stationed overseas and wasn't a part of our lives. He would just pop up once in a blue moon, buy us presents, fight with our mom, and disappear. My mom remarried a man who was an alcoholic and physically abusive. My mom and sister and I all were victims of his drunken rages at one time or another. Fortunately, my mom didn't stay in that marriage long, but she was having a hard time; so when I was about eight and Erika eleven, we went to live with my father and his new wife in Italy.*

*I was happy to finally be given the chance to get to know my father, but our stepmother did not seem to be keen on me and Erika. About a year after our arrival, Erika went back to live with our mother in Maryland, and not long after that, my little brother was born to my father and stepmother. I grew to love him dearly. However, it was made clear to me early on that my brother came first. While it wasn't his fault that he was favored and I was neglected, it set the tone for the rest of my time living with them. It turns out I was now in a family that was big on God and discipline but short on love for me. At least that is how I was made to feel.*

*When I was thirteen we moved to Virginia, and we joined a church where my father was a deacon and I was very active in the youth group. One thing I noticed early on is that the families of my friends at church weren't like mine. We argued and fought all the time, and I was such a bad kid; but everyone at church loved me and thought I was a great kid. I did very well in school, graduating from high school with an advanced credit diploma with the governor's seal on it. But at home I had one problem after another.*

*After countless power struggles, I couldn't stand living in that house anymore. I moved to Florida and lived with my mother and sister. However, after leaving such a strict and controlling household, I wasn't very receptive to anyone telling me what to do. I started off being fairly responsible; I got a job and gave my mom whatever money she asked for to help with bills. But I started to experiment with drugs—mostly marijuana and LSD—and I drank a little. I stopped going to church and started going out more with my friends. It wasn't long before I was immersed in the club and drug scene. Life became just working and clubbing and using and selling drugs. I didn't realize then the harm I was doing to myself and others. I was out of control—lost in a world I thought was giving me the freedom I craved.*

*The more I broke the law the more I viewed myself as on the other side of the law and the easier it became to do things I knew I shouldn't. The more I got away with breaking the law the cockier I became; I didn't think I could be caught. My low came at the end of 1995. I had recently lost my job because I showed up at work still messed up from the night before. I was so embarrassed. I was unemployed and using drugs heavily, mainly supplied by a "friend," Mark, who was stealing from the pharmacy at Eckerd drugstore, where he worked. Rocky, my best friend at the time, had had his life threatened by drug dealers to whom he owed money, so when Mark devised a scheme for the three of us to rob Eckerd and take care of our money problems, it didn't seem like such a bad idea. Armed robberies weren't my thing, but I was assured it would be easy and nobody would be hurt. As a testimony to how screwed up I was, I didn't even consider the psychological hurt our actions would cause, or the possibility of something violent happening. Little did I know*

183

*that many lives would be permanently altered by my decision to take part in the plan and to carry the gun. I believed it would be safest in my hands because I knew I wouldn't fire it.*

*The night of the robbery, we used cocaine, and then because we were too amped up, we swallowed valiums. It's amazing I could think at all. Mark was to drive the car, and Rocky and I were to approach the manager as he or she left Eckerd with the cash deposit bag. When I came out of the bushes and approached who I know now was Mrs. Sargeant, I was holding the gun at waist level. I said simply, "You know what this is, and you know what I want." Mrs. Sargeant handed me the bag. As I turned to look over my shoulder for Rocky, who wasn't there, the gun went off! I turned my head around and saw Mrs. Sargeant on the ground. I couldn't tell where she was shot. I ran. Mark and the car were gone. I was crying and running, dodging cars, police officers, helicopters. I managed to get home, where I told my mom everything. We found out that Mrs. Sargeant had died, and I was crushed. I was scared. I was so ashamed. I had taken someone's life, and I couldn't give it back.*

*I was arrested, and I confessed. To this day, I don't know how the gun went off, but it wasn't because I intended to pull the trigger. That doesn't mean I don't take full responsibility for Mrs. Sargeant's death, because I know that only I am to blame. All the poor choices I made prior to that awful night led to Tammy Wilson and her siblings losing their beloved mother and Mrs. Sargeant's husband losing his wife. While in county jail pending trial, I wrote a letter to the family, apologizing for my actions. I never heard whether or not they received it. I was so low because of all my victims and the prospects for my future. I just couldn't wrap my mind around how everything had gone so wrong. I prayed and at times read the Bible, but no real change had yet taken place in me spiritually.*

*I was convicted of first-degree murder and sentenced to life in prison without the possibility of parole. It hasn't been easy for me. It shouldn't be easy for me. One thing that has been a constant over the thirteen years I've been incarcerated is that I've encouraged those who are getting out to leave their criminal past behind, lest a tragedy happen and they aren't given any more chances. I try to show them all the people who are hurt by their decisions, using my own story as a prime example.*

*No matter how much I wish I could turn back the clock, I can't. I can only affect the present and the future. So I long ago resolved to live my life like I was truly sorry for what I have done. That has meant doing my best to grow and to help others. Over the past several years, God has used even this tragedy to mold me into the man he intends me to be. I know it will be a lifelong process, so even though I've come a long way, I have so much more room to grow. To have the opportunity after all these years to tell Mrs. Sargeant's family how sorry I am for the harm I have caused them is amazing to me. A couple of times after my conviction I asked my mother to try to track down the family so I could send a letter, but she was unsuccessful. The last time I asked her to try was on August 9 of this year. On August 25, my friend Jason, your son, asked me if my middle name was Ben. And you know the rest of the story, Mrs. Kent.*

*Something I wrote to Tammy Wilson—and I'll share with you here—is my deep desire to live the way I believe Jesus had in mind when he said that those who have been forgiven much love much.[7] I have been forgiven much by many, and as much as I would like to be free of these prison walls, I have resolved that I want God's will for me more. If this is where he intends for me to be, then I will serve him here to the best of my ability. My body is confined, but because of God's abundant grace poured out on me—someone who does not deserve it—my soul is at liberty. I have a peace in my heart as I seek to do the will of my Father. I will not allow Tonya Sargeant's death to be in vain.*

*Tammy Wilson closed her letter to me with these words from the Bible: "'For I know the plans I have for you,' says the LORD, 'They are plans for good and not for disaster, to give you a future and a hope.'"[8] I praise God that through you, Jason, and Tammy Wilson,*

*I have been given a renewed sense of hope for the future. Thank you
again. May God bless and keep you and yours always.*

> *Sincerely,*
> *Matthew Ben Rodriguez*

## Amazed by Grace

This remarkable story continues to unfold, and I can only stand amazed
by grace. A couple of weeks ago, not even a year since Matthew and
Tammy first exchanged letters, I received another note from Tammy:

> *Hi Carol,*
>
> *On the radio today I heard you being interviewed on the topic of
> hope for prisoners and their families. Thank you for continuing
> to spread the message, especially about forgiveness. It really is a
> powerful tool that is helping to defeat the evil in this world.*
>
> *Matthew and I write fairly often and are finding common safe
> ground. You facilitated that connection, and I thank you again.
> My family and I are all doing great. I want to visit Matthew soon.
> My two siblings and I are trying to schedule a trip to see relatives
> in Florida, and we hope to meet Matthew then.*
>
> *As you continue to travel and speak about your journey with Jason,
> I pray you will feel the Lord's presence and that he will keep you safe
> in his loving arms.*
>
> *Tammy*

Tammy and her siblings are living out one of the most challenging adventures I can possibly imagine. They are planning a trip to a
Florida prison to meet the man who murdered their mother. Talk about
the surprise of a lifetime! I believe they have come to understand the
truth of what Johann Christoph Arnold states: "Forgiveness is power.
It frees us from every constraint of the past, and helps us overcome
every obstacle. It can heal both the forgiver and the forgiven. In fact,

it could change the world if we allowed it to."[9] Adventure doesn't get much more exciting than this!

## A View from Eternity

When any of us comes to an impasse on our journey — an obstacle that changes our lives in disconcerting ways — if we keep our eyes and hearts open, we can find divine surprises worth discovering. For Gene and me and countless others, one of the greatest surprises is being empowered, right in the middle of our tight spots, to help others along the way.

Throughout this book, you've read stories of people who have faced a challenge and discovered how to mine for gold in the midst of their struggle. Their inspiring experiences of finding "the grace place" remind me that the surprise of adventure comes in many forms. Each of us faces a different "hard place," but if we allow it to bring us to the "heart place" where we lean into God's inexplicable favor and grace, we will find ourselves living in the middle of a miracle. Our circumstances may not change, but our perspective will. We will begin to view life through the lens of eternity.

Claudine Henry honestly shared her journey through postpartum depression when family and friends and even doctors didn't understand what was happening to her. She was in despair and planned to run away from home, but she discovered a way out of her hard place by learning to praise God and to choose hope over despair. Later, Claudine revealed the emotional devastation of being so financially needy that as her family approached Christmas, they had almost nothing in their cupboards. With great reluctance and embarrassment, she applied for food stamps. But what she thought was a "bottom" turned out to be far from it. Her example of finding joy and gratitude in her hard place gives me encouragement.

When Gail Knarr's husband, Brian, was arrested and charged with homosexual activity in a public park restroom, she never dreamed that something so devastating could result in anything but more humiliation and brokenness for her and her family. But in the midst of that toughest spot in their lives, Brian and Gail were showered with grace and continued to receive unexpected help and encouragement from their church family. Little did they know that in the midst of this humiliating experience they would experience an adventure of being showered with grace in the form of tangible help and compassionate community.

*Unemployment* is a word that frightens most of us because we anticipate not only financial hardship but also struggles with self-esteem and questions about whether or not God will take care of us or even cares about our dreams. Cathy Gallagher's story reminds us that this "adventure" can become a passage to a place of contentment. She is not in her dream job, but she has found the safety and security of being right where God wants her — and that's a safe place to be!

When Jill Gregory joyfully anticipated raising twin daughters, she never imagined that one of them would be born autistic. Jill's dreams for how Sarah and Kendall would grow up together are not turning out the way she anticipated, but by choosing thanksgiving over disappointment and self-pity, Jill and her family are embracing an adventure with God that is a positive example to everyone around them. Their story inspires me to hold on to hope even when nothing in my current situation changes in the way I would like it to.

Diana Pintar shared the story of her "long good-bye" as she waited day after day at her father's bedside, praying for him and waiting for him to pass into eternity. Her surprise was the joy she experienced in the midst of her grief, as God filled her heart and mind with a clear vision of her father — at home with the Lord, greeting relatives and friends who had gone on before him. Finally home!

The story of Tammy Wilson and Matt Rodriguez reminds me that saying yes to God and pressing into the Rock releases his grace, mercy, healing, and peace, which ultimately turns our journey into a grand adventure that is far bigger than we are. That doesn't mean the path in front of us will always be easy or enjoyable, but our story can be infused with a redemption we never dreamed possible.

The way our lives unfold is often outside our control, but we do have a decision to make when we are between a rock and a hard place. Joseph Campbell states, "The big question is whether you are going to be able to say a hearty yes to your adventure."[10] If we are willing to risk saying yes to God instead of no, our challenge can be transformed into an expansive adventure infused with meaning and grace. Rather than being an obstacle that ends our journey, it can become a new beginning.

My author friend Christin Ditchfield recently sent me this note:

*I'm praying for you that in the days to come the Lord will keep your vision clear and your steps sure as you climb the path he has ordained for you. It's not easy scaling those heights in the here and now; in fact, at times it feels treacherous. But the view from the top — from eternity's vantage point — must be fabulous.*

Now *that's* an adventure I don't want to miss!

## EXPLORING YOUR OWN GRACE PLACE

Adventure is something most of us look forward to in life. When we're young, it might be as simple as a trip to the mountains or a visit to an amusement park. But over time, our adventures tend to be defined less by geographical locations or thrills and spills and more by the joy of accomplishment and a sense of fulfillment. Our personal and spiritual adventures often take us down unanticipated paths on which we find obstacles that seem to stand in the way of our dreams. However, looking back in the rearview mirror of time often helps us see that what we once deemed a roadblock on our adventure led to a divine surprise on a purposeful and meaningful journey. Each barrier provided us with an opportunity to lean into the grace place and find a new kind of confidence and security.

1. Looking back on your childhood and young adult years, what was your most adventuresome experience? Did the presence of risk or danger make it more or less enjoyable for you?

2. Which of the following phrases best describes you?

   * I love to try new and challenging things, even if there's some risk involved.

   * I prefer experiences that provide predictable results and expected outcomes.

   * I dislike any experience that makes me feel frightened and out of control.

3. What is it about a personal or a spiritual experience that qualifies it as an adventure for you? Do such adventures often contain elements of risk or challenge that make you think twice before signing on? Think of an example in your life. What did you decide and why?

4. David was a flawed man, but he was also a great leader. As you read about him in this chapter, what part of his life did you identify with the most?

   ✦ An individual from humble beginnings who wound up with great opportunities

   ✦ Someone with everything going for him who allowed the enemy's temptations to take him down

   ✦ A person who knew he sinned greatly but also recognized that he was loved by God and that he was forgiven.

5. The story of Tammy Wilson and Matthew Rodriguez is an adventure that is still unfolding. When God brings people together in his timing, miraculous things happen. What part of this story impacted you the most, and why?

6. What shape does the challenge to "seize the day!" take in your life right now? Read the following Scriptures and summarize them in a way that helps you articulate the adventure God is calling you to live out, perhaps in very surprising ways!

   ✦ Jeremiah 29:11

   ✦ Psalm 32:8

   ✦ Joshua 1:9

   ✦ Proverbs 2:1 – 5

   Write a letter to God, telling him where you are in your journey toward "maximum security faith." List the divine surprises you have encountered along the way — even when you have been wedged into very tight spots. What unexpected treasures have you discovered, and how have you experienced God's mercy as you have said yes to him?

# The Ultimate Surprise

It was our first Christmas as a married couple — winter 1969. Our apartment was one of two units in a house that had previously been a funeral home. It was small but had the essential rooms — a living area, a small kitchen, a bedroom, and a bathroom. It was also in the right price range — cheap! We decorated it with a combination of garage sale items, not-so-lovely antiques, and family castoffs.

As the holiday season rolled around, funds were tight, but Gene and I budgeted a hundred dollars to spend on Christmas gifts for each other. We purchased an inexpensive pine tree from a local gas station manager, and my mother gave us ornaments, lights, and tinsel. That year we turned our lowly "funeral home apartment" into a magical holiday fairyland. Both of us managed to find several small sentimental gifts to wrap up for each other, but one day a package showed up under the tree that was larger than the others. The tag read: *To my gorgeous wife from the man who's crazy about you*. It was wrapped in shiny green paper with a big red bow on the top.

Gene watched as I picked up the package and shook it. "Hmmm — this looks very intriguing," I mused. "And it's wrapped so beautifully."

"I had help with that part, but I picked out this present all by myself. I hope you like it as much as I do!" He put his arms around me from behind and kissed the back of my neck, lingering as he enjoyed my keen interest in his gift.

The next morning he left for work early, and I had a couple of hours before my first commitment. Walking over to the Christmas tree, I picked up the mystery package and shook it again. Nothing rattled, and I was baffled by what might be in the box. I played with the bow and discovered I could easily remove it from the package and put it on again without causing any damage.

Suddenly, I was a child again, unable to wait for Christmas morning. I simply *had* to know what was in the package. I carefully pulled on the tape and discovered it was possible to pull the box out of the paper without ripping the fancy wrapping. Before I'd thought twice, I opened the box. I was delightfully surprised to discover my new husband had picked out a stunning "little black dress" for me with a matching coat. The coat had exquisite detail around the sleeves and collar. After scrimping to pay for four years of higher education, my clothing budget was nonexistent, and this ensemble was simply spectacular. I couldn't resist trying it on, and when I looked in the mirror, I squealed with pleasure. Apart from my wedding gown, it was the most elegant dress I had ever donned, and it made me feel like a princess.

After wearing my gift for another fifteen minutes while parading in front of every mirror in our apartment, I took it off and carefully placed it back in the box, guided it into the wrapping paper, secured the original tape, eased the bow back into position, and placed the package back under the tree.

On Christmas morning, Gene couldn't wait for me to open my present — and I was looking forward to seeing it again myself. As I pulled out the dress and coat I exclaimed, "Ohhhh! It's beautiful. What a *surprise*! (Well, it *had* been a big surprise a few days earlier.) It looks like exactly the right size. How did you find a gift that is so *perfect* for me? I absolutely *love* it!" And I did. It remained a favorite in my wardrobe, and it wasn't until several years later that I admitted to my juvenile pre-Christmas actions. Gene and I laughed about my inability to wait for the surprise and about the first "viewing" of the dress taking place in a funeral home.

Life seemed simple then. We were a young couple in love, with a desire to do God's work in this world and a commitment to live for things that matter. Life is more complicated now. We've had good times, but we've also had impossibly hard times. Our unthinkable circumstances have tested our faith, and our new kind of normal means challenging ourselves to make hope-filled choices every day. Some days are harder than others. We still want to live for things that matter and accomplish God's purposes with all the time and energy we have to offer. But we are more thoughtful, more transparent, and more compassionate than in days past. Those are good changes.

One of my surprises during the past year has been getting a glimpse into the heart of Tammy Wilson — the daughter of a murdered woman. Tammy's story has helped me identify more closely with the family of the man Jason murdered and to feel the depth of their loss and the ongoing grief over the absence of the one they love. Holidays are always the hardest time for me because that's when families get together. I am acutely aware of the absence felt at the Thanksgiving and Christmas tables of other families that have experienced the death or incarceration of a loved one. We are the walking wounded, impacted by an amalgamation of love, shock, anger, fear, hurt, and sorrow.

I know Jason feels the pain too. Just this week he admitted he is struggling more with depression than he has in the past several years of incarceration. But he also reminded me that he has a relationship with God today that is more intimate and transparent than ever before and that he experiences God's grace every day — even behind prison bars.

The same is true for me. And because of God's grace, I am blessed and surprised by a richer, closer, and more rewarding relationship with my son than I ever might have had if he weren't incarcerated. He has grown spiritually beyond anything I could have prayed for, and I have come to understand that grace shines brightest in hard, often dark places. I am learning how to forgive others quickly when I am wronged, lest I become a prisoner myself. I am less judgmental and more merciful, less stubborn and more giving. I like the new me better than the old me.

But every time I think I'm making it to a grace-filled plateau where this journey might get a little easier, I'm blindsided by my humanness. Last week I was putting in my four miles of walking (a new daily discipline this year), and I passed by the house of a neighbor. Several cars were in the driveway and others lined the street. Through the home's big front windows I saw people talking and laughing. A young mother was holding an infant in her arms while adoring grandparents looked on. Young children were outside playing tag, and others were throwing a Frisbee back and forth. The energy was captivating, and I realized I had happened upon a family reunion.

It took no less than another step for me to experience the pangs of jealousy, the realization that my life will not have the same opportunities for carefree gatherings that include my son when our family celebrates a graduation, a birthday, or a holiday. That is a harsh reality. Again I was reminded that each of us who walks the path of brokenness needs to *choose* how we will respond when the obstacles on our journey loom large or when the enemy tempts us to believe that there is no more reason to hope and no point in continuing to grow. Instead of brooding over my neighbor's blessings and my own losses, I started to pray for that family as I continued my walk. I prayed that they would not only have a joy-filled reunion but also be drawn to deeper faith in God and into more intimate relationships with each other. Before long I was no longer jealous because I was comforted by the infinite mercy and extravagant love of my Father God. I was leaning into "the grace place," and in that moment it was not hard.

When I got home, I settled into my favorite chair and picked up a devotional book I've been reading by Sarah Young. She often wrote in her journal after reading God's Word and meditating on his message to her heart. Her words remind me to cling to the Rock — God himself — and to appreciate the surprising gifts that are mine to discover every day if I keep my eyes open and my focus on eternity.

Approach each new day with desire to find Me. Before you get out of bed, I have already been working to prepare the path that will get you through this day. There are hidden treasures strategically placed along the way. Some of the treasures are trials, designed to shake you free from earth-shackles. Others are blessings that reveal My Presence: sunshine, flowers, birds, friendships, answered prayer. I have not abandoned this sin-wracked world; I am still richly present in it.

Search for deep treasure as you go through this day. You will find Me all along the way.[1]

I have been graced by a fancy package left on my doorstep by a friend and delighted by a sacrificial Christmas gift from a new husband. But these have not been my favorite gifts in life. The best ones have come disguised in suffering I would never choose, and they are priceless: the comfort of a friend who cries with me when my heart is breaking, the joy of watching my son growing deep in his faith, the opportunities to encourage people who are hurting, and the privilege of connecting people to the real source of hope: the Rock I cling to — God himself.

My loving God allows me to be honest, to voice my hurts and my questions. Sometimes I don't understand him at all. But if I didn't have him, then where would I go? To whom would I turn? I'd have no hope for the future — in this life or the next. I would give in to depression and despair. I would give up on everything and pull away from his touch. I would never experience his grace in my hard places. I would miss so much.

Recently I was reading the apostle Paul's letter to the early believers at Colossae, whom he referred to as "stalwart followers of Christ."[2] Gene and I continue to learn, along with our son, that we can remain faithful to our calling to follow Jesus and to find meaning in our lives, no matter what — and Paul sums up the reason why:

> The lines of purpose in your lives never grow slack, tightly tied as they are to your future in heaven, kept taut by hope.
> The Message is as true among you today as when you first heard it. It doesn't diminish or weaken over time. It's the same all over the world. The Message bears fruit and gets larger and stronger, just as it has in you.[3]

Whatever you are experiencing on your journey, no matter how tight the spot is in your life today or next week or next year, God's grace can make all the difference. He himself is the Stone in the road. Press into him, and open your eyes to divine surprises. And be reassured, as I am, by Paul's words to the Colossians:

> Not many of you have met me face-to-face, but that doesn't make any difference. Know that I'm on your side, right alongside you. You're not in this alone.
>
> I want you woven into a tapestry of love, in touch with everything there is to know of God. Then you will have minds confident and at rest, focused on Christ, God's great mystery. All the richest treasures of wisdom and knowledge are embedded in that mystery and nowhere else. And we've been shown the mystery![4]

That, my friends, is the *ultimate* surprise!

# Acknowledgments

In the spring of 2008, my sister, Jennie Afman Dimkoff, e-mailed me the words of Romans 9:33, adding simply, "This verse is for you." The words written by the apostle Paul to the early Christians in Rome were originally spoken by Isaiah, the Old Testament prophet. Century upon century had passed, yet Isaiah's prophetic metaphor for Christ's disruptive and wondrous presence in the midst of the human drama would prove to be as relevant and dynamic as ever. The verse in my e-mail inbox became the catalyst for the book you now hold in your hands.

A week after Jennie drew my attention to these ancient words, I sat on a plane next to a man I had never met. With my laptop computer open on my tray table, I was pondering Romans 9:33, typing potential titles for a book based on this verse. Suddenly my seatmate spoke up. "Excuse me for reading your screen," he said, "but it looks like you're trying to come up with a title for a book. How about *Between a Rock and a Hard Place*?" A few days and several flights later, I met in Colorado with my dear friend and trusted editor, Traci Mullins — and the rest is now history. Traci immediately caught the vision for what the message of this book could be, and eighteen months later, *Between a Rock and a Grace Place* was complete. Traci helped me craft the manuscript with her courageous and creative ideas, extraordinary editorial skills, penetrating questions, genuine compassion, and demand for excellence. More than twenty years ago, she came alongside this fledgling young speaker and helped me hone my writing skills. Traci is a gifted wordsmith, and I am grateful for her expert coaching and for her enduring friendship.

As an author, I want my books to be more than a chronicle of my own journey, so I am thankful for the courageous and inspiring people who share their poignant and surprising stories in this book. I am indebted to Claudine Henry, Brian and Gail Knarr, Cathy Gallagher, Jill Gregory, Diana Pintar, Tammy Wilson, and Matthew Rodriguez. Their authenticity challenges me to lean into "the grace place" so I won't miss the divine surprises in the middle of the road I travel.

I am grateful to my son, J.P. (Jason Paul) Kent, who wrote letters from his prison cell with gut-wrenching honesty and transparency. I see in him a hard-won humility, forged in the kiln of human suffering and heartfelt repentance as he submits to God's authority in his life. I weep for his losses, but I rejoice over his deepening spiritual maturity.

My husband, Gene, shared his own journey freely, contributing excerpts from his private journals. He regularly reminded me to take the time to enjoy long walks and beautiful sunsets, the comfort of family and friends, and the pleasure of great cups of coffee while I invested months of work on the manuscript. Gene's tender love for me and for our son makes every day a better day.

Our ministry intercessors, led by Kathy Blume and Sandi Banks, continue year after year to bathe all our efforts in prayer. My mother, Pauline Afman, and my sister, Bonnie Emmorey, have been of invaluable help as our outreach to inmates and their families through Speak Up for Hope continues to expand. How thankful I am for my family members and friends and their ongoing encouragement to us and to our son!

I am deeply grateful to Cindy Lambert, vice president and associate publisher of trade books at Zondervan, for championing this book throughout the publishing process. Her passion for the message of *Between a Rock and a Grace Place* has been unwavering, and her outstanding editorial skills helped me and Traci polish the manuscript as we approached the finish line. Thanks, too, to the publishing team at Zondervan for putting their heartfelt enthusiasm and marketing skills into promoting this volume and everything it represents to our family and to the ministry God has graciously sustained and blessed in the midst of our heartaches.

Finally, I extend heartfelt thanks to my readers. I pray that you will continue to find renewed hope and greater awareness of God's grace in the middle of your own tight spots in life. If you have your own story to share of discovering a "grace place" in the midst of a difficult challenge, I would be honored to hear your story. You are welcome to e-mail me through my website at www.CarolKent.org.

> And now to him who can keep you on your feet, standing tall in his bright presence, fresh and celebrating — to our one God, our only Savior, through Jesus Christ, our Master, be glory, majesty, strength, and rule before all time, and now, and to the end of all time. Yes.*

---

\* Jude 1:24 – 25.

# NOTES

CHAPTER 1: **Grace in the Hardest of Places**

1. Hebrews 11:1 NIV.
2. Psalm 71:14 NIV.
3. Lamentation 3:19 – 23 NIV.
4. To contact Claudine Henry personally or regarding speaking engagements, please write to her at claudine@heartstringministries.com, or visit her website at *www .heartstringministries.com.*
5. Job 6:2 – 3.
6. Job 2:9.
7. Job 2:10.
8. Job 6:11 NLT.
9. Job 9:21 NLT.
10. Job 17:7.
11. Job 17:11 NLT.
12. Job 42:12.
13. Patrick Overton, "Faith," in *The Leaning Tree* (St. Louis, Mo.: Bethany, 1975).
14. Job 2:9.
15. Job 2:10.

CHAPTER 2: **Angels in Disguise**

1. Luke 10:25.
2. Luke 10:27.
3. Luke 10:29.
4. Luke 10:25 – 37.
5. Paraphrased from the *Life Application Study Bible: New International Version* (Wheaton, Ill.: Tyndale House; Grand Rapids: Zondervan, 1988, 1989, 1990, 1991), 1695.

6. Luke 10:36.

7. Luke 10:37 NLT.

8. To contact Brian and Gail Knarr, please e-mail them at bgrknarr@comcast.net.

9. Psalm 34:18.

10. Matthew 25:35 – 36.

## CHAPTER 3: Longing for a Better Life

1. http://www.gaia.com/quotes/Billy_Graham

2. Quoted in Ann Coppola, "Simple Place for a Simple Man," November 5, 2007, *http://www.corrections.com/news/article/16995*.

3. Facts based on Philippians 3:5 – 6 NIV.

4. Acts 9:4 – 5 NLT.

5. Philippians 4:22.

6. Read the whole story in Acts 16:19 – 28.

7. 2 Corinthians 12:7 – 10.

8. *Merriam-Webster's Collegiate Dictionary*, eleventh edition.

9. Philippians 4:11 – 13.

10. Hebrews 13:5 NASB.

11. Philippians 4:6 – 7.

12. 1 Timothy 6:6 – 7 NLT.

13. Matthew 6:34.

14. To contact Cathy Gallagher, please e-mail her at CathyCLG@aol.com, or to request information on having her speak at your event, write to Speak Up Speaker Services at speakupinc@aol.com.

15. C. S. Lewis, *Mere Christianity* (New York: Macmillan, 1981), 115.

16. Philippians 4:6 – 7 NLT.

## CHAPTER 4: The Secret Power of Gratitude

1. Psalm 126:3 NIV.

2. To contact Jill Gregory, please e-mail her at gregoryfam1994@yahoo.com.

3. 2 Chronicles 20:4.

4. 2 Chronicles 20:6.

5. 2 Chronicles 20:9, 11 – 12.

6. 2 Chronicles 20:17.

7. 2 Chronicles 20:21.

8. 2 Chronicles 20:21 NLT.

9. 2 Chronicles 20:24 NLT.

10. 2 Chronicles 20:25 NLT.
11. 2 Chronicles 20:32.
12. 2 Chronicles 20:33 NLT.
13. 1 Thessalonians 5:16 – 23.
14. Jackie Windspear, quoted in Kerry and Chris Shook, *One Month to Live: Thirty Days to a No-Regrets Life* (Colorado Springs: WaterBrook, 2008), 212.
15. 1 Thessalonians 5:18 NASB.
16. R. P. C. Hanson, quoted in Marcia Ford, *Essentials for Life* (Nashville: Nelson, 2010), 118.

CHAPTER 5: **Unexpected Kindness**

1. *Merriam-Webster's Collegiate Dictionary*, eleventh edition.
2. To contact Claudine Henry personally or regarding speaking engagements, please write to her at claudine@heartstringministries.com, or visit her website at *www .heartstringministries.com*.
3. Genesis 37:3 – 4 NLT.
4. Genesis 37:19 NIV.
5. Genesis 39:4 – 5.
6. Genesis 39:7 NASB.
7. Genesis 39:21 – 23 NLT.
8. Genesis 41:16 NLT.
9. Genesis 41:39 – 43.
10. Genesis 41:51 – 52.
11. Genesis 50:19 – 20 NLT.
12. Genesis 50:21 NLT.
13. Amelia Earhart, quoted in Karen Weekes, *Women Know Everything!* (Philadelphia: Quirk, 2007), 237.
14. Carol Kent, *When I Lay My Isaac Down* (Colorado Springs: NavPress, 2004), 76.

CHAPTER 6: **Why Do You Weep?**

1. Helen Keller, *The Story of My Life* (New York: Doubleday, 1903), 182.
2. Based on information in Luke 8:2.
3. Matthew 27:55 – 56.
4. Ann Spangler and Jean E. Syswerda, *Women of the Bible: A One-Year Devotional Study of Women in Scripture* (updated and expanded ed.; Grand Rapids: Zondervan, 2007), 389.
5. John 19:25.

6. Matthew 27:46.

7. Mark 15:47 NLT.

8. John 20:2.

9. John 20:11.

10. John 20:13.

11. John 20:15.

12. John 20:15.

13. John 20:16.

14. John 20:16 – 18.

15. Matthew 28:1 NIV.

16. Ken Gire, *Intimate Moments with the Savior* (Grand Rapids: Zondervan, 1989), 132.

17. William Vander Hoven, quoted in Albert M. Wells Jr., *Inspiring Quotations* (Nashville: Nelson, 1988), 103.

18. Psalm 23:4.

19. Psalm 16:11 KJV.

20. Ephesians 1:18 NIV.

21. To contact Diana Pintar, please write to her at thenextstep@mac.com; regarding speaking engagements, visit www.SpeakUpSpeakerServices.com.

22. *Merriam-Webster's Collegiate Dictionary*, eleventh edition.

23. Tim Hansel, *You Gotta Keep Dancin'* (Elgin, Ill.: Cook, 1985), 133.

24. Hebrews 12:2 NLT.

## CHAPTER 7: A Different Kind of Liberty

1. Isaiah 50:4.

2. "That's why we can be so sure that every detail in our lives of love for God is worked into something good" (Romans 8:28).

3. Psalm 119:32 NIV.

4. John 13:8 NLT.

5. John 13:8 NLT.

6. John 13:9 NLT.

7. John 13:34 – 35 NLT.

8. John 13:37 NLT.

9. John 13:38 NLT.

10. Matthew 26:69 NIV.

11. Matthew 26:70 – 75.

12. Matthew 16:18.

13. Lewis Smedes, *Forgive and Forget: Healing the Hurts We Don't Deserve*, new ed. (San Francisco: HarperSanFrancisco, 1996), 133.

14. Catherine Ponder, quoted in Tian Dayton, *The Magic of Forgiveness* (Deerfield Beach, Fla.: Health Communications, 2003), 87.

## CHAPTER 8: Dwelling in the Grace Place

1. If you would like to help fund the workbooks for this course, tax-deductible contributions can be made at www.SpeakUpforHope.org.

2. Available through the American Association of Christian Counselors, www.AACC.net.

3. Read David's entire story in 1 Samuel 16 – 1 Kings 2.

4. Acts 13:22 NLT.

5. Psalm 51:1 – 10 NLT.

6. Psalm 51:10.

7. Luke 7:47.

8. Jeremiah 29:11 NLT.

9. Johann Christoph Arnold, *Why Forgive?* (Farmington, Pa: Plough, 2000), 158.

10. Joseph Campbell, quoted in James Randall Miller, *Thoughts from Earth* (Victoria, B.C.: Trafford, 2005), 38.

## EPILOGUE: The Ultimate Surprise

1. Reprinted by permission. *Jesus Calling*, Sarah Young, 2004, Thomas Nelson, Inc., Nashville, Tennessee. All rights reserved.

2. Colossians 1:2.

3. Colossians 1:5 – 6.

4. Colossians 2:1 – 3.

# About the Author

Carol Kent is an international public speaker and bestselling author. Founder of Speak Up for Hope (a prison ministry), Speak Up With Confidence (a communications training seminar), and Speak Up Speaker Services (a speakers bureau), Carol is an expert on public speaking, on writing, and on encouraging people to hold on to hope when life's circumstances turn out differently from their dreams.

Carol speaks weekly all over the U.S. and has carried her inspiring messages to South Africa, Germany, Bulgaria, China, Korea, Hong Kong, Guatemala, Mexico, and Canada. She regularly appears on a wide variety of nationally syndicated radio and television broadcasts, and she sits on the advisory boards of MOPS International and the Advanced Writers and Speakers Association. Her articles have been published in a wide variety of magazines, and she is the author of numerous books, including *When I Lay My Isaac Down*, *A New Kind of Normal*, *Becoming a Woman of Influence*, *Mothers Have Angel Wings*, *Secret Longings of the Heart*, *Tame Your Fears*, *Speak Up With Confidence*, and *Detours, Tow Trucks, and Angels in Disguise*.

Carol and her husband, Gene, live in Lakeland, Florida.

To book Carol for speaking engagements,
call 888 – 870 – 7719.

For more information,
go to www.CarolKent.org.

Speak Up for hope

*is a nonprofit organization that seeks*
*to live out the principle of Proverbs 31:8 – 9:*

"Speak up for the people who have no voice,
for the rights of all the down-and-outers.
Speak out for justice.
Stand up for the poor and destitute!"

**Vision:** To help inmates and their families adjust to their *new normal.*

**Mission:** We exist to provide hope to inmates and their families through encouragement and resources.

# Goals

## 1. Encourage

- Provide ideas for resources needed by inmates, including electronic equipment, educational materials, large-print Bibles, books, greeting cards, and sports equipment.
- Provide resources for prison visitation areas, such as games, cards, coloring books, and crayons for use by prisoners and their families.
- Offer resources by Carol Kent.
- Provide information on Boxes of Hope for organizational projects.
- Provide information on Jump Start Bags for prisoners upon their release, including practical items needed for a new beginning.

## 2. Counsel

- Offer counseling by licensed counselors to inmates' families to help them understand and cope with their current situation.
- Offer information packets to the prisoner and his or her family once sentencing has occurred to assist with legal and practical issues.

## 3. Educate

- Assist churches or individuals with information on working with prison chaplains, prison education departments, wardens, and probation officers.
- Provide information on materials available that will teach inmates important life skills, including practical money management, communication skills, and effective marriage and parenting techniques.

It is the goal of Speak Up for Hope to give hope to the hopeless, encouragement and strength to the weary, reparation to marriages that have been torn apart by incarceration, and mental, spiritual, and physical stability to the children of prisoners.

We pray that people all over the world will begin speaking up for those who cannot speak up for themselves. As people become the hands and feet of Jesus to "the least of these," something miraculous happens. As we choose to get personally involved by giving, volunteering, and praying, we are transformed from the inside out as we model for others how to become hope givers.

*Carol Kent*

CAROL KENT, cofounder

*Gene Kent*

GENE KENT, cofounder

For more information on the variety of ways in which you can be involved in Speak Up for Hope, please contact:

**Speak Up for Hope**
P.O. Box 6262
Lakeland, FL 33807-6262
www.SpeakUpforHope.org
888.987.1212

Make tax-deductible contributions payable to Speak Up for Hope or donations can be made online at www.SpeakUpforHope.org

Speak Up for
hope

# How Individuals
# Can Get Involved

Most of us are overwhelmed by how many needs inmates and their families have, so it's hard to know where to start. If everyone reading this page would do *one thing*, we could accomplish a lot. Here is a list of needs Speak Up for Hope has on an ongoing basis. Prayerfully consider where you want to begin:

- books of first-class postage stamps that are sent to inmates
- new greeting cards and envelopes (birthday, Christmas, friendship, Mothers Day, etc.) that are given to inmates to send to their families
- DVD teaching programs on marriage relationships, financial management, parenting skills, and Bible studies that can be sent to prison chapel programs
- new books and Bibles we make available as gifts to family members of inmates
- inspirational CDs and DVDs we send to chapel libraries.
- gasoline gift cards for spouses of inmates

- black, size large T-shirts for women who are turned away when they come to visit their loved ones because their apparel doesn't pass the dress code
- a twenty-dollar donation for the cost of sending one of Carol's books to an inmate or to the family of an inmate

Contact us at Bonnie@SpeakUpforHope.org for information on the following additional opportunities:

- joining the prayer team of Speak Up for Hope
- receiving a quarterly e-newsletter on our current projects and needs
- writing to an inmate who has no family support
- volunteering to teach GED or college-level classes at a prison in your area
- organizing a group of volunteers to fill "Boxes of Hope" for families of inmates

Thank you for making a difference!

# How Organizations and Churches Can Get Involved:

### 1. Plan a "Boxes of Hope" project.

Speak Up for Hope fills boxes for wives and moms of inmates that include comfort items, encouraging reading material, inspirational CDs, and notes to let the recipients know they have been prayed for by name. If your church or women's ministry group decides to sponsor a Hope Box mission project, you can do this in connection with a seasonal event such as a mother-daughter banquet, a retreat, harvest supper, or Christmas event, at which time donations can be collected. Ask people who are attending your event to bring any of the following items: small stuffed animals; Bibles and Christian books; praise and worship CDs; coffee mugs; individually packaged specialty coffees, teas, or hot chocolate; journals; stationery; bookmarks; small photo albums and picture frames; small facial tissue boxes; books of stamps; phone cards; encouraging refrigerator magnets; bath products such as hand and body lotion, shower gel, and bubble bath; pedicure supplies, and scented candles. Contact the Speak Up for Hope office for an address where these items can be sent for distribution.

## 2. Participate in a prison visitation park project.

A major need in most prisons is for games, word puzzles, and coloring books that will enable children who are visiting their parents an opportunity to have fun and meaningful interaction with their incarcerated mom or dad. If your organization or ministry decides to host a prison visitation park project, keep in mind that all items should be new and in their original packaging. Any of the following items are appreciated: board and card games, educational flash cards, coloring books and crayons, activity books, word-find books, crossword puzzle books, children's storybooks, Bible storybooks, Bibles, and devotional books.

Note: Some individuals in your group may not have time for collecting and packaging, but they may be able to help financially with the cost of mailing boxes to the Speak Up for Hope office or to the individual recipients. Make tax-deductible contributions payable to Speak Up for Hope. Donations can also be made online at www.SpeakUp forHope.org.

To contact the Speak Up for Hope office for more detailed information and for an address where current shipments can be sent, e-mail Bonnie@SpeakUpforHope.org.